MOVE IN
AND
MOVE UP

MOVE IN
AND
MOVE UP

by E. A. Butler

———————————————

THE MACMILLAN COMPANY

Library of Congress Catalog Card Number: 76-95180

FIRST PRINTING

The Macmillan Company
866 Third Avenue, New York. N.Y. 10022
Collier-Macmillan Canada Ltd., Toronto, Ontario

Printed in the United States of America

CONTENTS

INTRODUCTION

NOT long ago the city of New York launched an investigation of so-called "executive counseling" firms. Acting license commissioner Joseph L. Forstadt estimated that these companies did a $25-million-a-year business in New York City alone. I would conservatively estimate that these same companies, and others, gross another $25-million-a-year outside New York, in cities across the nation. Most of this $50 million is wasted. P. T. Barnum in his heyday never swindled the suckers more successfully than these so-called experts, who charge as high as $2800 to tell a man how to change himself and his career in pursuit of that big brass ring called success.

I take pride in having played a part in stimulating this investigation. More than six months earlier, in my syndicated column "On the Job," I had attacked these man-eaters and called on businessmen to drive them out of the business community. The response I received from dozens of American cities made it clear that I was not by any means writing fiction. But it dawned on me then that there was another, more meaningful side to this exposé. If honest, hardworking men were willing to pay $50 million for bad advice, it signaled a very serious need in the modern business world, which was not being met. That was when I decided to write this book. In it I hope I can share with these searchers for intelligent advice the insights I have acquired from eighteen years of huddling with presidents and board chairmen, discussing the intricacies of finding the right men for demanding jobs. I write in the hope that I can save a new generation of executives from the mental and financial anguish inflicted on too many men by these shyster career counselors.

At the same time I want to make it clear that this book will go beyond the corporation in its discussion of success. I don't believe the corporation or the corporate training program is the be-all and end-all of business life. I think there are dozens of other ways a man can move up in the business world, even though he may never get his name in gold letters on the corporate door or be up to his ankles in deep-piled prestige carpet. I have been moving up since the age of fourteen, and only a small fraction of this time has been spent working for large corporations.

At that beardless age I started selling peanuts and soda at tobacco auctions in my native North Carolina, and pretty soon I had a company with a half dozen younger kids working for me. I am as proud of this move as I am today of E. A. Butler Associates, my management consulting and executive recruiting company, with offices in major U.S. cities.

On the side, I run a major ski resort and lodge in the Adirondacks, and I participate as a silent partner in a half dozen other businesses. Moving up, then, in my terms, is moving *into* the kind of success a man needs to make his life satisfying. It can be a very modest success—$10,000 or $20,000 a year—or it can be the stupendous variety that a friend of mine is determined to achieve. He wants to be worth $100 million before he dies. I don't see anything wrong with either one of these wishes. This book will tell you how to achieve both of them.

MOVE IN
AND
MOVE UP

BEGINNER'S LUCK

CHOOSING a job is the most important decision a man makes in his life. It is more important than choosing a wife. A man's work—his frustrations and achievements, the emotional and financial rewards he derives from it—shapes him far more profoundly than any other single influence in his life. We are only beginning to realize the enormous influence of the job *on* the man. In the last decade social scientists and psychologists have accumulated a staggering dossier of facts about the emotional problems people face because they are round pegs in square-hole jobs. According to the National Association of Mental Health, there are 2 million alcoholics in industry. Other surveys estimate that 80 to 90 percent of men fired in an average year lost their jobs because of personality problems, not incompetence. I know, of course, that a percentage of these men brought their emotional problems with them when they began work, but my

eighteen years in industry has persuaded me that an astonishing portion of such men are deeply unhappy because
they chose the wrong job either in the very beginning of
their career or when they were in middle management, or
because they momentarily lost their grip on the very top
rungs of the ladder and chose the wrong executive suite.
The story of a man's working life is really a drama of choices.
It lasts far longer than the two and a half hours of make-
believe we see on the commercial stage. But when we cut
away the web of minutiae of which every man's life is
woven, we find at the core these basic moments of decision. Let us take a look at some typical moves—and their
consequences.

I met George Bailey ten years after he had "chosen"
his first job. I put the word "chosen" in quotes because that
was the way he described it. Actually his first job had chosen
him. George was one of those countless thousands who suc-
cumb to the siren song of the corporation recruiter at the end
of their senior year in college. With a blizzard of statistics,
promises, and idyllic photographs of modern plants and
happy, smiling employees, the recruiter took George by
storm. Oh, he listened to a few other recruiters whose pitch
was not quite so persuasive, but this represented the sum
total of time and effort George put into his search for a first
job.

Result: George, who was born and educated in the East,
found himself in a two-year training program in a small Midwestern city. He did not do well in the training program,
largely because he didn't like small-city life. His wife, whom

he had married just after graduation on the strength of the excellent starting salary the company offered, liked it even less. An energetic extrovert, George felt baffled and confined by the big company's rigid personnel policies and long-established—and I should add successful—ways of doing business. The company, probably not much more enthused about George than he was about them, decided to slot him in sales promotion. He wound up strapped to a desk, grinding out new-product letters, and drifted largely by attrition to the head of this section of the promotion department. By this time his salary had risen to five figures, as part of the company's standard annual increases. Years passed while George presided with steadily decreasing satisfaction over younger new-product letter writers. Because he was unhappy, he became edgy, authoritarian. He had a number of ugly disputes with new men and it was clear to his superiors that a lot of the trouble was his fault. At home George began bickering with his wife, had fits of depression, and began drinking heavily on weekends.

One day George Bailey woke up and a realization enfolded him, permeated his whole body like a great clammy, clutching hand—he was beginning his tenth year with the company. Ten years—a fourth of his working life— had sped past and where was he? He was a lower middle executive doing a job he hated in a company he hated in a city he hated. That was when George came to me for advice.

"Maybe it won't make you feel any better, maybe it will," I said, "but you have made one of the commonest mistakes in the business world. You assumed that you chose the job and therefore you had to stick with it. You felt your own prestige was involved and, to quote the deadliest phrase in business, the money was good."

"I'm thirty-two years old," he said. "Is it too late for me to change?"

"No," I said, "but another five years and it would have been too late."

So George Bailey began a drastic overhaul of his career. He moved back to the East, took a sales job at a reduction in salary with a smaller company in the same industry, and in two years had passed his old salary. His mental and physical ailments, his troubles with his wife vanished. His vigor and enthusiasm won friends and influenced all sorts of executives as well as customers and I heard confidentially not long ago that he is currently considered one of the bright young men to whom his company is looking for leadership ten years hence.

Then there is Ted Grant, who was not fortunate (or unfortunate) enough to go to a college where the corporate recruiters swarm each spring. Ted had to find, not be found. How did he go about it? He wasted fifty dollars on a printer who gave him 500 gaudy copies of his résumé and mailed them out to 500 companies. Of course, he told himself, he was looking for a job. But actually he was hoping that a job would look for him. He wanted that same warm, mothered feeling George Bailey got when the recruiter showered him with praise and slick blandishments. Ted Grant might just as well have taken his list of 500 companies, put it up on a wall, wrapped a blindfold around his eyes, and plunged a pin into it. He could even have added a jackass's tail to the pin to make the comparison complete. Luckily for him, however, he did not get a single answer from his 500 résumés.

Another grim tale concerns a young man named Edward Glazier. On the basis of some rather good marks in mathematics in high school, a guidance counselor had steered him into an engineering course in college. Gifted with more than a little native intelligence, Glazier had done well enough on the academic side, but the longer he toiled to acquire the engineer's skills, the less enthusiasm he felt for his future profession. His father and mother, neither of whom had gone to college, meanwhile thrilled to the prospect of their son the engineer. They regarded him as a combination Edison and Steinmetz and at family gatherings were constantly marveling over his scientific prowess. After four years of engineering, however, Eddie Glazier was sick of it. But could he dare to walk out on it now? Could he turn his back on all that training, those acquired skills that guaranteed him a good salary?

No, he decided. He could not do anything so extraordinary. Cruel fate had decreed him to be an engineer. He would grit his teeth and do the job. Hoping for the best and secretly fearing the worst, he went to work for a big oil company.

Charles Fleming had a different problem. His father was the owner of a very successful cement company. Practically from the day he was born Charles was groomed to inherit the company. Ignoring his son's inclinations and talents, which were very much inclined to a career in science, the father enrolled him in a business course in college and, mixing bribery and authority in about equal shares, cajoled Charlie through the curriculum and inducted him into a personal training program that would prepare him to become a captain of the cement industry.

Charlie may be consoled by the thought that he too is not alone. Although the number has diminished in recent years, parents who choose their children's careers for them—and children who let their careers be chosen—are still high on a list of major sources of blunders for job beginners.

But the basic folly, which I have seen repeated in a dozen guises, is rooted in reluctance or inability to admit a mistake. So you took the wrong college course, chose or were chosen by the wrong company, let your father or mother maneuver you into a career you never really wanted. The day, the hour, the minute, if possible, that you realize it, get out. Take to the hills, if necessary, Alaska or Australia, Siam, if you don't want to look people in the eye and admit the boner—which is by far the best course. Don't waste time meditating on whether you should be loyal to a parent who has paid for your education or a company that has invested a year or two in training you. In the long run you will make either or both of them happier by moving now. Above all, it will guarantee you a decent shot at happiness. Admitting a mistake is the first step toward acquiring that toughness of hide and spirit which a good executive must possess.

All right, you say, now we have heard the negative. We know how not to do it. Turn us around and get us moving, at least theoretically, the right way. Let's go.

There are three vital ingredients in choosing a first job—time, thought, and action.

Time is the most neglected ingredient. People spend four, five, six years acquiring an education, yet will rarely devote even two weeks to investigating the practical considerations involved in the choice of any job. General Electric wants to take you to Schnectady for its training program. I personally think Schenectady is a nice town, but you might hate it. How are you going to get at least an idea of your reaction to the place? You can question people you know who have been there, but the best thing to do is to go there yourself. Spend the weekend, walk around, talk to people. Are two days and a few hundred dollars in travel expenses to be compared with the time and money you have put into your education? Isn't this small investment worth it (assuming GE is one of your final job choices) to safeguard the far larger investment? Yet it is very rare for a college man today to make such an investigation. He allows himself to be contented with the recruiter's slides and glowing descriptions of the company. I say no intelligent man should go to work for a company until he has personally visited its offices and factories.

This takes time. But if you take life seriously, if success and wealth are goals you honestly believe you have the talent to achieve, then such a search is worth every second you invest in it. I say it should begin the day you select your major in college. Weekends, vacations should be devoted to it, especially in your senior year. Making the scene at Fort Lauderdale or Bermuda may seem a lot more important when you are on campus, but a trip to Duluth, Minnesota, to check out a very good job possibility may make you a lot happier and richer five or ten years hence.

So again I say go see the company, talk, if possible, to some of the executives, get some idea of the kind of life you will be leading. Without this kind of knowledge you may find yourself on the kind of fool's errand George Bailey chose.

Thought involves something more than an analysis of the company itself. Your goals, your family background must also be considered in a job choice. What do you want out of life? Maybe a million dollars does not interest you. Maybe you prefer the rewards of civic virtue, the fulfillment that comes from serving others. This is not a primary emotional experience in business, however much executives may talk about their company's services to the economy and the community. But this kind of psychological analysis can be carried somewhat further. Do you chafe under restrictions and rules or do they provide you with a useful sense of security? Does the idea of operating as a lone wolf alarm or excite you? How hard do you want to work? Are you healthy enough to put in a ten- or twelve-hour day? Do you plan, practically from graduation day, to have a wife at your side? If so, what are her goals, her attitudes toward long hours, separation from her family?

The answers to these questions are terribly important. If rules and regulations are your cup of tea, a big company may well be the best for you. On the other hand, if rules make you break out in hives, think twice about committing yourself to one of our corporate giants. Do you plan to build your career around a single skill, such as accounting or engineering? You can learn a tremendous amount in a big company. In such fields their standards are high, their men in the upper echelons are the best that money can buy. Or

are you more interested in acquiring a broad, fairly diversified business experience in your early years? Unquestionably
then, a small company can give you much more. In the small
company you will usually have a chance to perform a variety
of tasks, shoulder a diversified pack of responsibilities. You
can broaden yourself much faster, but your depth may be
somewhat lacking.

If your choice is the small company, the question of
personality—yours and the company's—becomes a very important concern. Are you surprised to learn that the company
has a personality? It has. It usually flows from the one or
two men at the top. Even sizable companies and some
corporate giants have very definite personality differences,
but among the bigger boys the differences are not felt or
seen as keenly because a single man takes much longer to
make an impression on the larger mass, usually with a longer
tradition of habit and policies. In a small company the man
on top may be a hard-driving order giver, a martinet who
delegates responsibility reluctantly. Or he may be a salesman who is out charming the rest of the industry and expects
those at home minding the store to make their own decisions.
For the beginner, such fairly general concepts of company
personality are usually enough on which to make a judgment. Only if you sense a direct clash between your habits
of mind and the company's ways of doing things should you
weigh them seriously in the balance of your job decision.
But the company's personality is nevertheless an important
concept to retain in your mental inventory for later job
decisions.

Action is the last ingredient, the one that converts into

capital the time and thought you have invested thus far. Let me illustrate with a story from my own experience.

When I began looking for my first job, I was immensely stimulated by a book, *The Power of People,* by Charles P. McCormick of the McCormick Spice Company in Baltimore, Maryland. McCormick was one of the pioneers of the multiple management or committee system of running a company. He argued persuasively that he had discovered a marvelous new kind of industrial democracy that created true team spirit as well as a productive, profitable enterprise. I had already done a good bit of reading on various theories of management and McCormick's book convinced me that his system was the wave of the future. I then went to the library, found out everything I could about the company— the cities in which it operated, how it distributed its products, the backgrounds of its chief executives. Standard & Poor's Industrial Index, Who's Who in America, Who's Who in the East, Who's Who in Commerce and Industry supplied most of this data. The banker father of a friend was good enough to get me a Dun & Bradstreet report on the company's profit picture, assets, and liabilities. Everything checked out extremely well. The company was solidly established, showed a steady profit, and maintained an encouraging interest in growth. I made up my mind that this was where I wanted to start my business career.

I got on a train and went to Baltimore. Hat in hand, I politely presented myself to McCormick's personnel department and proceeded to tell them why I was the man they should hire.

They said, "That's very interesting but I'm sorry, we don't have any openings at present."

I said, "I would like to speak to Mr. McCormick."

In his book, Mr. McCormick had boasted that among the prime advantages of multiple management was that it removed burdens from the president. His door, he declared, was always open and he had ample time to see everyone who wanted to see him.

When the personnel office tried to discourage me, I marched upstairs to Mr. McCormick's office and repeated my request to his secretary. She too was not encouraging. I proceeded to quote relevant passages from Mr. McCormick's book. I told her why I thought the company was missing an opportunity if they failed to hire me. She told me Mr. McCormick was terribly busy. I said I'd wait.

I sat in Mr. McCormick's outer office for a day and a half. Finally he saw me. I told him why I wanted to work for his company. He was impresed by my knowledge of the company as well as by my perseverance. He sent me on a round robin of interviews to a dozen other executives, all of whom gave me the kind of grilling my brashness undoubtedly deserved. (I should add, however, that my *manner* was not brash. I did not pretend to be a know-it-all nor did I sell myself as a miracle man. I presented myself as nothing more nor less than what I was—young, intelligent, energetic, and intensely interested in McCormick and Company.) After looking me over for several days, McCormick and his executives made an unprecedented decision: they hired me without a recommendation from the personnel department.

To go out of channels in such an old, established company was very unusual and they made it clear to me that I was going to have to prove myself in spades. That did not bother me. I had made my point. I had gotten the job.

I do not for a moment maintain that this is the only way to land your first job. My tactics—appearing on the doorstep of the company, camping in the president's office—are incidental. Tactics should be improvised to the given situation. But the principles involved in my approach—*time* taken to investigate the company, *thought* about what the company had to offer me, *action*, landing a job with them.

Consider the difference between this approach and the 500 résumés idea. It is the difference between the sharpshooter and the machine gunner. It is not that I am prejudiced against résumés. Far from it. Later in this book I will devote an entire chapter to the preparation of them. But the résumé should be integrated into your tactics, it should be specific, a wedge to open your selected company's door a little wider.

In my experience I have found that a well-written letter to a company president or some other key executive is far more likely to open doors for a beginner than a résumé. A letter is you in action, putting your best foot forward, explaining yourself and simultaneously demonstrating your ability to communicate, to draft ideas, discuss issues. In the letter you should ask for an interview with the president or one of his executives. In many if not most companies you will be referred to the personnel department, where you will have to submit to some psychological testing. In a later chapter we will discuss how to clear this hurdle. However long the personnel men probe and poke you, continue to ask and eventually to demand the interview with the men at the top.

You should bring to bear in this interview all the time and thought you have invested in preparing for this moment of truth. The impression you make, your success or failure in landing the job will, of course, depend on some factors beyond your control. But let me assure you, the executive will be impressed and possibly even delighted by the interest you have taken in his company. He has probably invested years in the creation of this company. You have bestowed the accolade of your attention on it. It is the kind of flattery that not many men can resist. If there are any openings to be distributed, you can be certain that you have a leg up on the average applicant who has simply forwarded his résumé or appeared under the aegis of a campus recruiter.

Let me be frank and say that this advice is far more geared to a job beginning with the small and middle-range companies earning between $5 and $100 million a year. General Motors, General Electric, and other such corporate giants hire a small army of men each year and it would be physically impossible for executives to see them all, or even a modest percentage of them. But again, frankness compels me to confess my doubts about beginning one's career with these corporate giants. When it comes to a choice between depth and breadth of training, I would advise breadth, at least for the young man. Twenty-eight to thirty-five are the prime years to acquire depth. By then the average man has a much more mature grasp of his goals, and a much clearer idea of what he can and cannot do. No matter how much time and thought you put into preparation for the beginner's choice, the early years of a young man's career should be regarded as tentative, exploratory, basically a learning experience.

There you have my credo for beginners. *Time, thought, action.* My substitute for beginner's luck.

THE RÉSUMÉ

WHETHER you are in the beginning, middle, or upper level of the executive world, how you make contact for a new job can make or break your career. The two basic tools are the letter and the résumé. I insist that both are equally important. To the average man, however, the résumé is the really vital tool. Unfortunately it is also a mystery, which many people think is beyond their power to compose. Much of the money devoured by shyster career counselors is justified to their victims by the preparation of flowery, elaborate résumés, which they print on vellum paper and mail out by the hundreds. Unfortunately vellum is just as easy to throw into the wastebasket as any other kind of paper.

Two things to avoid in your contact letter are attempts at humor or a breezy, offbeat style aimed at making you sound "different."

A typical letter of this sort may read like this:

Hello there!

This letter should acquaint you with Frank Fremle, a personable guy with mountains of ambition and an eye peeled for a sales position of high caliber. Frank did his cheering for Eastern College. His studies led to a B.S. in accounting. (Postgraduate courses in business and law while working.) He was a "B" student and participated in such activities as president of Dinkum House, a fifty-man social fraternity, business manager of the yearbook, and freshman baseball.

At Jacobs, O'Hara & Co., Certified Public Accountants, Frank worked on financial statements and had the opportunity to coordinate such projects as budgets and costs.

Now Frank is twenty-five. He has a broad educational background and a great deal of business experience, combined with two important ingredients—the ability to make friends easily and a strong and sincere desire to sell. What more does one need? Would you like to know more about Frank? Then write

> Mr. Frank Fremle
> 524 Green Street
> Blankville, New York

I almost forgot to say . . .

> Sincerely

Almost inevitably the letter reader will conclude from this letter that Frank Fremle is a happy soul with a somewhat empty head and a talent for breezy phrases—and not much else.

A letter written in a businesslike manner, simply stating your reasons for desiring an interview with a particular person, will win you more interviews than any other type of approach.

Direct your correspondence to a departmental executive or personnel director, addressing him by name. Give valid reasons for your desire to explore employment possibilities in a specified department of his particular company, or as a general trainee. If there is an opening for an employee in that department or for personnel expansion in general, and if he is therefore willing to consider hiring you, he will contact you directly. It is also desirable to send a copy of the same letter to the personnel director if the original letter was sent to a department head. Should the department head have no opening in the department you suggest, and if he is extremely busy, your letter may die or be waylaid in his office. Also remember that there are companies with as many as 300 employees who do not have personnel departments. A letter sent only to the attention of "Personnel Director" may fall into the hands of the company officer who happens to be handling this phase of personnel operation. He may not be directly aware of the needs in all departments.

It is far better to obtain the names you need from Poor's Register of Directors and Executives. This book is published annually and is kept up-to-date. Included in its alphabetical listing of approximately 100,000 companies is information pertaining to products, numbers of employees, annual sales volume, headquarters, and names and biographical notes concerning directors and executives.

When you do not have any previous long-term experience it is better to say so than to imply the contrary in your letter of application. Most young men have a tendency to inflate their activities and responsibilities. Such inflation is quite obvious to the experienced executive.

Be brief in stating your desire for the type of work you are seeking. For a beginner to attempt to stretch his letter into a full page about summer jobs, extracurricular activities, and the like is in no way beneficial to him. While these activities may be vitally important to you, it is more than possible that they are inconsequential and uninteresting to the executive reading your letter.

An example of one acceptable letter for an applicant, an executive trainee, is:

Dear Mr. Jensen:

After a careful consideration of the fine things about your company, I have decided that I would like to associate myself with it.

I am twenty-five years old, married, and willing to relocate if you wish. I am a graduate of Columbia University, where I received a B.A. degree in 1957, with a major in ———. I have fulfilled my military obligation.

After evaluating my desires for a future in industry, I feel certain that it is advantageous for me to explore the possibilities of joining an organization such as yours.

Will you be kind enough to allow me time to state my reasons in person?

Respectfully,

Later, when you become an experienced executive, you should maintain a résumé which gives the salient features of your background. Its use obviates the need for a long letter in great detail which may be confusing and time-consuming to the reader. The letter accompanying the résumé should be clear and brief. (It is surprising how many executives, who should be able to write a good letter, send in a poorly written effort.)

For example you might write as follows:

Dear Mr. Thompson:

I have known of the activities and reputation of your company for many years. At the present time I wish to make a change in my business affiliation. I am in a position to select the kind of company that I desire to remain with. Therefore I am applying to you for an interview to explore the possibilities of a position with your company.

I am enclosing a résumé of my activities and salient points of background. If after you review this you desire a personal interview, I shall be glad to make myself available at your convenience.

Sincerely,

Like the letter, the résumé that is brief and well organized and gives important facts without beefing up is the one that is most apt to get attention and secure an interview. Remember that people considering applicants at an agency or counseling service are accustomed to receiving some twenty-five to fifty résumés daily. If you talk to a personnel director or an officer of a fairly good-sized company, you will find that he too is swamped. My executive search company gets about 300 résumés a week. Anyone reviewing résumés is a normal human being looking for shortcuts to save time. You would do the same thing. That is why the succinct, hard-hitting résumé is the best.

How long? I am not a believer in the absolute restriction to a single page, but everything above two pages is almost certainly going to be unread and a brochure of four to ten pages is a totally futile gesture.

Should you write your own résumé? Absolutely yes. But I see nothing wrong with soliciting advice from a professional. Even a draft of a résumé, based on information you give him, may be helpful in organizing the main outlines of your career. But the individual should make an effort to improve and alter this outside composition.

Let's first take a look at how not to prepare a beginner's résumé. The first example has too many words under certain of the headings.

CONFIDENTIAL RÉSUMÉ

George P. Hamilton   Home Telephone: PO 6-4426
884 Welton Drive
Clinton, New York

PERSONAL DATA

Age: 22   Height: 6′   Weight: 185 lbs.
Single

EDUCATION

University of Rochester B.S., June 1969
Business Administration

EXPERIENCE

June–September 1968 *Hamilton Manufacturing Co.– Utica, N.Y.*
Duties: During the summer of 1968 worked in my father's office as a sales correspondent. The job entailed: receiving inquiries about various products our company manu-

factured; obtaining necessary information; writing sales letters, enclosing various brochures; discussing the products in question.

Other activities were: handling customer complaints, which necessitated discussing complaints with production heads and sales personnel to determine the justification of each complaint.

It is my belief that I learned a great deal about diplomacy and proper customer relations from this job.

June–September 1967 *County Construction Company– Albany, N.Y.*

Duties: I was very active in athletics and, as a result, engaged in heavy construction work to keep myself in top physical condition. I believe very strongly that an active mind requires a strong, healthy body.

June–September 1966 *Avalon Lifeguard Association*
Duties: I was a lifeguard on the beach at Avalon.

I feel that I gained nothing significant in this position, aside from the fact that I had a wonderful time.

More detailed information available on request.

Far better is the following effort, in which the young man states succinctly what he's gotten out of his modest experience thus far.

CONFIDENTIAL RÉSUMÉ

George P. Hamilton   Telephone: PO 6-4426
884 Welton Drive
Clinton, New York

PERSONAL DATA

Age: 22   Height: 6'   Weight: 185 lbs.
Single

EDUCATION

B.S., June 1969 University of Rochester
Business Administration

EXPERIENCE

June–September 1968 *Hamilton Manufacturing Co.–
Utica, N.Y.*
Duties: Replying to inquiries regarding products manufactured; writing sales letters accompanied by brochures concerning our products; replying to customer complaints after consultation with department heads and sales personnel.

It is my belief that I learned a great deal about diplomacy and proper customer relations in this position.

June–September 1967 *County Construction Company–
Albany, N.Y.*
Duties: Participation in heavy construction work.

This job was taken to keep myself in trim for college athletics on my return to college in the fall.

June–September 1966 *Avalon Lifeguard Association*
Duties: All activities connected with a position as beach lifeguard.

Note: I shall be glad to furnish any additional information you may wish.

The résumé of a man in middle management will naturally take up more space. But again, the aim should be succinct summary. Here is a good example:

CONFIDENTIAL RÉSUMÉ

Albert D. Palmer   Home Telephone: DE 2-1132
1102 Maple Street
Norwich, Connecticut

THE RÉSUMÉ

Age: 34   Height: 5'11"   Weight: 178 lbs.
Married   2 children

EDUCATION

Mass. Institute of Technology   Graduated 1947—B.E.E.—
   Engineering
Columbia University   Graduated 1955—M.B.A.—
   Bus. Admin.

EXPERIENCE

June 1957 to Present   *American Electric Corporation—*
New London, Connecticut
December 1968 to Present
Title: Division Product Manager (washing machines, dish-
washers, etc.)
Duties: Responsible for the development of complete
marketing and merchandising program for this division.
Responsible for the current profit position for the corporation, on these products as well as on new product development. Also responsible for the continual evaluation of
current distribution policies and for recommending improved programs.

February 1968–November 1968   Title: Merchandise
Manager
Duties: Assigned the responsibility under the Product
Manager for the development of complete merchandising
programs on the division's products—the areas of sales training, product display, advertising and promotional theme,
and pricing. Also responsible for the presentation of this
complete program to the field organization.

May 1966–January 1968   Title: Asst. to Division Manager

Duties: Staff position assisting the Division Manager in administrative duties. Supervised Sales Department budgets and kept the Division Manager informed as to the financial status of operations. Handled special assignments in the sales area and submitted reports and analyses on how the division's operation could be improved.

September 1964–May 1965
Duties: Attended Columbia University, Graduate School of Business, under the sponsorship of American Electric as part of the company's middle-management program.

January 1960–April 1964   Title: Sales Engineer
Duties: Responsible for rendering complete commercial service to accounts in utility and consulting engineering fields. Handled broad application and sale of full range of company's electrical apparatus products including generators, transformers, motors, etc.

September 1957–October 1958
Duties: Assigned to Vestibule Training Program of American Electric.

Professional Societies
Licensed Professional Engineer, State of Connecticut

Résumés of advanced executives are even more detailed. Again, however, verbal restraint should be the goal. But the restraint should not be so total that the résumé becomes merely a dull list of duties performed. Always remember a résumé is a selling tool. It isn't enough merely to list the things you have done. The emphasis should always be on what you have *achieved.* Above all, never simply list a job in one-line, throwaway fashion. For example, I recently saw the résumé of a rather gifted writer, who was looking for a position in public relations. He had spent the last five years in government service, writing speeches for cabinet-level officials. He spent most of his time talking about this aspect of his past in the résumé. When he got down to his previous experience in the business world, he simply said:

1953–55—Senior writer, IBM internal magazine

After talking this experience over with him and pointing out that, valuable as his government experience was, it would not carry its apparent weight in the business world, we revised this section of his résumé as follows:

1953–55—Senior writer, IBM internal magazine. Traveled as far as California to do stories on plants and personalities. Interviewed supervisors, salesmen, vice-presidents. Worked closely with public relations vice-president and other officials on preparation and final editing of stories.

It's evident that the executive who reads this revision will say to himself: "This fellow knows how to handle himself inside a company. He's dealt with top people. I'm not taking on some weirdo who got a government job through political pull."

It is vital, in every résumé, to try to anticipate the psychology of the man or men who will read it. If you are trying for a job in an advertising agency, you can add a little more zip to your descriptions. If the job on which you are drawing a bead requires considerable teamwork, don't hesitate to emphasize your past accomplishments in getting along with people. At the same time, nothing hits a résumé reader harder than facts. As you travel through the business world, keep a record of your record. Copywriters, commercial photographers, and artists maintain a portfolio of their productions, from which they can select material at a moment's notice when they are job hunting. Far too many young businessmen have no record whatsoever of what they accomplished when they worked for General Motors. It is especially hard in a big company to compile a record of one's productivity or achievements. But it is vital to make an effort to do so.

Don't be shy either about claiming for yourself accomplishments which, to be literally honest, belong to a team. Everyone who reads a résumé expects the writer to be puffing himself a little. The sad fact is, so many men don't know how to do it *effectively*. If your labor-management team reduced plant disputes 50 percent in two years, by all means get it into your résumé. If the sales promotion department in which you were a humble enlisted man, grinding out copy, reduced its budget while the company doubled its sales in a given fiscal year, don't hesitate to mention that either. Describe yourself as playing "a leading role" in this achievement. Maybe it was your suggestion or suggestions that enabled the department to cut its budget.

Always mention a promotion within a given job experience. If you went from salesman to assistant sales manager in two years, point it out briskly and clearly. Then tell what you did as assistant sales manager, even if the sales manager would probably make similar claims. Again, the résumé reader will subtract the difference automatically. But he will say to himself: "This fellow can't be a dud if he was on a winning team."

Never, on the other hand, put a negative statement into a résumé. If you were fired from a job, it is no disgrace. We will discuss later in this book how to handle it candidly. But résumés and letters are door openers. Remember you are competing with those forty or fifty other men whose résumés land on the executive reader's desk each day. Remember he's only human, and he's looking for ways to eliminate interviewees who are probably going to waste his time. He works on probability, not certainty, because that's all he has to go on. As sure as sunrise and sunset, if he sees a confession of defeat, an admission of failure in your résumé, it will be one of the first to go into the "sorry, no openings at the moment—don't call us, we'll call you" file. The same thing goes for someone who has had a past history of mental illness or alcoholism. Don't under any circumstances mention it in your résumé. Such information can be handled candidly and honestly in an interview, when you are there to supplement the words and present a convincing, healthy demeanor to the man who may hire you. Remember that a résumé is only a very faint image of your real self. You can't hope to present in a page or two the complex circumstances which created your problem, or the authenticity of your recovery. A résumé is a kind of photograph, and as anyone who has ever paid for a formal photo knows, you naturally take the best-looking version of yourself that comes off the film, at least on the safe side of blatant pretty-boyness.

27

If you have trouble accentuating the positive in your résumé, it may help to talk over your job experiences with a friend who has shared some of them. Often a friend is much more objective about your accomplishments than you are, especially when you are feeling depressed and uncertain, as many job seekers do. Sometimes, when a man is out of work, the past suddenly takes on a gray, dreary, treadmill appearance, in which nothing good or even mediocre ever happened. An hour's reminiscence with a friend on the telephone, even if it's long-distance, can bring back an awful lot of sharp recollections. If you've left your previous job in a reasonably friendly manner, don't hesitate to go back to your former colleagues and get some hard facts about profits and production to add backbone to your self-portrait. Best of all, as I've already suggested, a man should keep a general résumé up-to-date, not only because it can be useful in an emergency, but because it gives everyone invaluable perspectives on his career and progress. If you have been on a job two years and you haven't one positive statistic to add to this résumé-in-progress, you might well start worrying about the future. I'm even in favor of young people collecting material for a résumé the moment they decide on a career goal. Don't hesitate to ask your summer job boss for a letter summing up your accomplishments and put it in the file. A sentence or two, or even a striking phrase drawn from it, can add impact to a first job résumé. I am aware that a lot of people may react negatively to such an approach. It is amazing how many people in this world don't want to admit they are ambitious. In fact, I sometimes wonder if the ability to admit and act on ambition is not the difference

between the successful man and the going-nowhere medi-
ocrity. The intelligent businessman is, believe me, never
disturbed to see signs of ambition in a job prospect. Ambition spells hard work to him, and that is the kind of man he
is looking for.

One other résumé hint worth pondering: These days,
corporations are all caught in a rather frightening profit
squeeze between ever higher taxes and ever more demanding unions. If you can get into your résumé some evidence
that you are a man who thinks in terms of profits, if you
are what I call somewhat crudely "a buck smeller," you will
have a leg up on those forty or fifty competitors whose
résumés the mailman delivers with yours. Don't talk about
the bonuses you got, emphasize the profits you made for the
company. Get that word "profits" in there as often as possible, without seeming obvious.

To go from the psychological to the mundane, and at
the risk of seeming obvious, I will remind you of a fundamental. Every résumé should be individually typed. No
carbons. Above all, no mass-produced mimeographed,
Xeroxed, photocopied, or printed versions. These only
expose you as an individual who is soliciting everyone and
who has given no special attention to the particular company
to which you are applying. You *must* remember that the
reactions of a company are as sensitive as those of a person.
I repeat, every company likes to feel that you are approach-
ing them because you are genuinely interested in them,
and in them alone.

Also, every résumé must be properly prepared, mech-
anically speaking. Typographical errors and poor grammar

should be nonexistent. This is worth stating, because I have seen all too many résumés where misspellings abounded and grammatical lapses were permitted to pass uncorrected. Such boners are invariably fatal. In some ways they are worse than an admission of those negative statements, such as getting fired, which I maintain should be banned as a matter of policy.

Perhaps the best reason for a freshly typed résumé with each job application is the inspiration it may give you to revise your résumé to fit the type of company to which you are applying. Always reshape a résumé to coincide with a company's immediate interests. In a constantly changing world, a résumé should be a flexible tool, not an immutable work of art.

STYLES IN SUCCESS

IF I were between the ages of twenty-one and twenty-five I would not go into the work I am doing today. The management consultant–executive recruiting field has become crowded (and I might add there are a dismaying number of frauds and phonies in the crowd). No, if I were starting out today, I would do what I did fifteen years ago. Swim against the tide.

The man who succeeds is the man who thinks, who calculates, who gives himself the best possible odds. Which does not, of course, guarantee success. But it makes it a lot more probable. And a large part of thinking your way to success involves prediction.

Eighteen years ago there were anguished screams from business about the need for engineers. Young men poured into engineering schools. And within five to six years, engineers were a glut on the job market. Today the pendulum has swung the other way. There is a genuine scarcity of talented, creative engineers. You may hear people tell you that nobody wants engineers. But they are echoing experiences eight or nine years old. There are always a lot of people around who lag that far behind the decision makers.

The same thing is true in the sales field. Companies are having terrible trouble recruiting salesmen from the college graduates of recent years. The word "salesman" has a faintly derogatory ring; it conjures up images of slapping backs and telling corny jokes. Now is the time for the really smart young men to enter sales. In a field of mediocrities, he will rocket to the top at double, triple the normal pace.

When I say this I am not asking anyone to do anything that is ethically or emotionally repugnant to him. On the contrary, the man who goes into sales will soon be laughing at his fraternity brothers, whose image of the salesman lags ten, perhaps twenty years behind reality.

Sales is rapidly becoming the focal point of the modern corporation. As one company president said to me the other day, "Anybody can make the stuff. But it takes brains to *move* it."

Salesmanship today requires imagination as well as energy, shrewd, decisive intelligence as well as personality. Modern salesmen fight, not for the single sale, but for control of a market. This requires a plan of campaign, a new way of communicating with customers, an ability to anticipate what the competition will do. The man who shows the boys on top that he can handle these multiple challenges is a cinch to move up fast.

Best of all is the man who combines sales know-how and an engineering background. He is the ideal who makes company presidents really salivate.

Today the man who does not plan a career with one eye on change is planning nothing for himself but trouble. According to a speaker at a recent conference on consumer credit, 60 percent of the 150,000 people who now hold supervisory positions in this industry will be replaced by computers in the next ten years. Another expert predicts that by 1975 there will be 50,000 industrial robots in action, with television eyes and an ability to remember and correct their mistakes. On the other hand, there is a tendency to get infatuated with the idea of newness and forget that older industries and older job skills are still going to be in the picture. Television did not kill off the movies any more than radio killed off newspapers or planes killed off railroads.

Change modifies industries far more often than it destroys them, and the man who understands these modifications and rides with the crest of the wave is the man who moves up. In banking, for instance, the man who can use computers is hot, in public relations, it is the man who can work with minority groups effectively and organize public interest programs for training the poor.

A friend in a position to know told me the other day, "The chemical industry is ten years behind in recruiting." The paper industry, one of the oldest in the country, is currently undergoing a quiet internal revolution. It used to be a maxim that paper executives had to start out at the bottom and work their way through all the jobs in the mill.

33

Now for the first time the paper industry is reaching out for skills that aren't taught in mills, but in graduate schools of business. A smart young man can take these facts and build them into a lot of career momentum.

Another important thing to remember is the value of new combinations. Look through your paper's classified ads on Sunday. I can almost guarantee you will see at least a half dozen examples of this kind of newness. I tried it the other day, and here are a few I found:

> Electronics manufacturer needs manager. Should have engineering and advanced administration degree.
>
> Manufacturer of air pollution control equipment needs engineers for sales and management.
>
> Wanted: health physicist. Broad experience in atomic energy field, plus ability to handle labor and community relations problems.

One of the most successful men I know graduated from engineering school in the early 1950s, then got himself a law degree. His friends thought he was crazy, but he is now making over $50,000 a year as an expert in the field of international patents. He foresaw the global nature of postwar business and its fantastically expanding technology. He prepared himself for a need that was, people now realize, predictable. But only my friend and a handful of others took the time to figure it out.

Think change, by all means. But don't see the future in terms of the totally new. It's a lot more complicated. The men who unravel the complications will be the winners of tomorrow.

This is, of course, by no means the only way to swim

against the tide. I remember the day I shocked an audience of young college men out their socks by telling them, "Open a retail store!" They looked at me as if I had really lost my marbles. They stopped laughing when I told them Joe Ehrenreich's story.

In 1931 at the very bottom of the first drop of the Great Depression's roller coaster, Joe opened the Penn Camera Exchange in New York. Through those lean years he grew steadily. He devoted time and attention to studying customers, finding out what they wanted and getting it for them. By 1950 the store was a $2-million-a-year business. More and more camera company executives paid quiet visits to Joe Ehrenreich to get his advice on marketing new products or putting some adrenalin into old ones.

Then, in 1953, into the Penn Camera Exchange walked a representative from the Nippon Kogaku Company of Japan, looking for ways to merchandise their photo equipment in this country. "It started out to be an intellectual exercise," Joe Ehrenreich says modestly. "But pretty soon I was thinking about it day and night, and by the time I developed a program I also decided I was the man to carry it through."

Ehrenreich went to Tokyo for intensive talks and in 1954 he formed a company today called Ehrenreich Photo-Optical Industries, Inc. It is the exclusive U.S. distributor for all types of cameras and optical equipment for seven major Japanese firms, and currently handles the largest dollar volume of all the Japanese cameras sold in the United States.

"Joe Ehrenreich," says a knowledgeable executive in a

rival firm, "is primarily responsible for the fact that Japanese cameras now outsell German cameras in this country."

Though his rise from managing a store to president of a $25-million-dollar-a-year company would seem breathtaking to most people, Ehrenreich insists that his roots, his know-how, are still in the Penn Camera Exchange. His experience there was the basis for the startling advice he gave Nippon Kogaku about how to enter the American market. Other importers had told the Japanese that they must forget quality and produce mass quantities at minimum prices. Ehrenreich told Nippon to do just the opposite. He took them into the professional photogaphic market, arguing that the pros, always open-minded and eager to find improved equipment, were the opinion leaders in the camera field and the group to convince of Nippon's superiority.

Ehrenreich persuaded crack photographers such as David Douglas Duncan and Carl Mydans to try Nippon's cameras. They liked them and spread the word. Building on their endorsements, Ehrenreich more than doubled sales in a single year.

Meanwhile he was building his own company slowly, as a small starter should. He began with a staff of four. He handed out franchises with the X-ray vision of a man who could see holes in a retail setup at a glance.

Today his company has 300 plus employees in five separate divisions, marketing not only cameras but high-priced military and scientific optical equipment. In 1963 he was cited by the Government of Japan as the single United States businessman most responsible for pioneering Japanese photographic imports in the United States—the first time the Japanese Government ever bestowed international trade honors on a foreign business executive.

Ehrenreich is still growing, because the man himself is still growing. He loves to spend an occasional day behind the counter to keep in touch with what people are thinking. Retailers like him because he is considered the most "dealer-minded" man in the entire camera and optical field.

Joe Ehrenreich himself insists there is nothing unique about his success story. It is something that any American can do, thanks to the opportunities which this country gives a man willing to think hard and work harder.

Ehrenreich, of course, moved out of his retail store and formed his own company. This is not the only way a man in a retail business can move up. As you will find out in the course of this book, I am fond of puncturing myths. But for a long time I have hesitated to attack the biggest myth of all—that only a man who sits in an office with a carpet on the floor, has a secretary at his beck and call, and wears a shirt, a tie, and the latest-cut suit can be called an executive.

It just isn't true. I can show you a dozen men who do none of these things yet are performing (rather than conforming) executives. Essentially an executive is a manager, and these men are doing one whale of a job managing complex enterprises. They also have something else in common—they are all in the franchise business.

Whoa! I can practically hear you snorting. Are you trying to tell me that the little guy and his wife who run the local Dairy Queen are executives? Probably not. Every field has its enlisted men and its officers. The franchise field currently has some of the biggest opportunities for officers.

There are some 400,000 franchises in operation around the country, and they account for more than 70 billion in goods and services annually. You see their names everywhere. Midas Muffler, Chicken Delight, MacDonald's Hamburgers, Beltone Hearing Aids. Big as the field has grown, it is still hampered by the Mom and Pop image. Only a few shrewd, energetic types know that a man with executive talents can acquire not one, but two, three, a half dozen franchises when he proves he has the know-how to run them, and in no time can find himself owning a million-dollars-a-year business. At a recent convention, the Mac-Donald Hamburger chain asked how many of its franchisees were millionaires, and eight people raised their hands.

Franchise profits are remarkable, often running to 15-20 percent of gross income. A few even report profit margins of 30-40 percent. This does not mean that the dollars grow like bananas and just have to be picked off the trees. The hours are invariably long, and the problems are often formidable. It can also be lonely. The franchisee had to make most of his decisions without an executive board to reassure him. But he can get advice and help from the parent company.

Franchisors pick their prospects very carefully today, usually insisting on an eight- or ten-week training program, where they study a man's aptitude as well as give him basic information. The would-be franchisee ought to be equally cautious. There are still some shady operators in the franchise business—phonies who sell you $750 or $1000 worth of cheap equipment and vanish into the night. They can be checked in advance through the Better Business Bureau or the International Franchise Association, which is trying hard to weed them out. Boston College has a center for the Study of Franchise Distribution, which is also helpful. The school's co-director, David B. Slater, sums up the field in a sentence. "The potential is tremendous."

Maybe you're the type who doesn't particularly want to leave his hometown. Not everyone is crazy about the idea of rushing off to New York, Chicago, or San Francisco. At the same time, you have that good, healthy, old-fashioned American desire to make money. Quite regularly now when young people ask me to suggest a good bet that would answer these two preferences, I reply, "Stocks and bonds."

This almost always brings a squawk of protest. But don't you have to live in New York? I promptly produce my wise man's (forty-two-year-old) smile and answer, "Not anymore."

Few people realize that Wall Street and Main Street have become practically synonymous. Stocks and bonds have become a national business and you don't have to live in New York to work on Wall Street any more than you have to live in Schenectady to work for General Electric. Programs for registered representative trainees recommended by the New York Stock Exchange are given in colleges in eight large cities—Boston, Chicago, Los Angeles, Miami, New York, Philadelphia, St. Louis, and San Francisco. Evening courses are given in related areas of accounting, salesmanship, marketing and advertising. Private consulting and training firms have recently entered the field too.

As for growth, it would be hard to find another industry that can boast of tripling its volume in ten years. In 1950 2⅓ billion shares were listed on the New York Stock Exchange. In 1960 it was 6½ billion, and in 1970 12½ billion. Shareowners have zoomed from 8½ million adults in 1956 to 17 million in 1962 and 25 million in 1970. In five recent years the number of employees in brokerage firms which are members of the New York Stock Exchange jumped from 60,000 to 90,000.

Significantly, a recent publications by the New York Stock Exchange on careers in the industry describes a typical registered representative—salesman to you and me— at work in Cleveland. A public school, liberal arts graduate, George Abrams took a six-month training course and passed a test on security analysis and brokerage procedures before he won his registered representative title with a major Cleveland firm. The RRs constitute about a third of all the employees in the securities industry—the largest single group. George has a number of clients, some with large holdings, others with small. He keeps track of their stock, warns them about mergers or unfavorable reports, and generally stays on top of the market for them. He also handles investments for nonprofit corporations such as universities.

From ten to three-thirty, when the market is open, his day can be feverish as buy and sell orders flow through his hands. Frequently, after the market closes, he will visit clients at their offices or in their homes. One man may want

some advice on how to revise his portfolio to get more cash
out of it. Another man wants to go into business and needs
advice on which half of his stock to sell. George makes a
fair number of these calls in the evening. He spends other
evenings studying market reports and client portfolios, long-
and short-range forecasts, and similar material. He enjoys
his work. The market is a fascinating creature once you
begin to study it.

If George continues to do well, he can look forward to
becoming a branch office manager. There, with bonuses and
a slice of the office gross, he can easily make $30,000 a
year before he is forty. He can also look forward to
building up a very healthy portfolio of his own. If he
works hard and creates a real following among his clients,
George can, if he is so inclined, switch to another, perhaps
smaller firm and become a partner with a proportionately
higher share of the profits. Dozens of these young firms have
sprung up in recent years in small cities and suburban
towns. The revolution in electronics communication puts
them almost as close to Wall Street as somebody operating
around the corner at 1 Broadway. A spokesman for the Stock
Exchange admits, "A small firm situated in a town of thirty
of forty thousand population may show a healthier profit
than a competitor ten times its size in a large city."

This very shrewd spokesman adds, "If a broker's career
is your objective it may be easier for you to build up a
clientele in your hometown. It could well be that what you
are looking for is right under your nose."

Even if you are inclined toward large corporations and
don't have much appetite for sales, there are smart ways to

move. One I call looking for the unconventional in the obvious. Not long ago I had lunch with A. J. D'Arcy of the Union Carbide Corporation. Mr. D'Arcy is vehement about the total ignorance among the young about his own field, purchasing. "Of all the career paths a young man might take, purchasing offers one of the best possible opportunities to rub elbows with decision makers on the middle-management and top-management levels," he says, "both inside and outside the company."

He is right, of course. The purchasing man is not cooped up in one department. He is a high-powered interdepartmental operator. I have often noticed how common it is for a man moving into the vice-presidential zone to have a purchasing tour in his early experience.

In a big company like Union Carbide, a purchasing executive in his early thirties could be responsible for spending anywhere from $10 to $30 million a year. As Mr. D'Arcy points out, these figures easily represent the total sales of more than a few sizable companies.

Best of all, purchasing gives a young executive a chance to step into the ring and test and hone his skills in decision making and in negotiating.

Yet ask the average college graduate what he thinks purchasing involves and you get a dismaying vision of buying rubber bands, typewriters, and stationery. They know absolutely nothing about the purchasing man as a decision maker with an in-depth technical background. Mr. D'Arcy likes to tell about one Union Carbide purchasing agent who received an order for an especially high-purity chemical. He had the buying knowledge to recognize that a commercially available purity was much cheaper; he had the technical knowledge to know that it would do the job, and finally, he had the skill in human relations to persuade the requisitioner to try it. Result: a 15 percent saving each year.

No wonder purchasing agents' salaries run in the $12,000 to $20,000 range. A director of purchasing or vice-president for purchasing often makes as much as $50,000 a year. When you consider that a manufacturing company spends anywhere from thirty to fifty cents out of every dollar of income for materials and services, the purchasing agent becomes one of the major sentinels of business profit.

"Every dollar saved through astute purchasing at Union Carbide," Mr. D'Arcy says, "is the equivalent of selling five dollars more in products. If the purchasing department can improve its performance by even one percent, it's the equivalent of $10 million a year added to the company's pre-tax net."

What do you need to make it in this tough league? At Union Carbide and other complex scientifically oriented companies, a candidate should come prepared with a technical degree and can expect a two- to three-year training program in production, engineering, field purchasing, or research and development before moving on to major buying responsibilities.

But it's well worth the time invested. For one thing, there's no need to fear that a computer will short-circuit your purchasing career. As Mr. D'Arcy likes to point out, a computer doesn't have initiative or tact. Above all, it doesn't know how to say "Why?"

"Once a man learns to ask that question," Mr. D'Arcy says, "he's on his way to becoming a first-class purchasing executive."

Purchasing is closely allied to another field which is currently producing more corporate officers than any other business discipline. Among them: Robert McNamara, former Secretary of Defense; Frederic G. Donner, chairman of the board at General Motors; Harold S. Geneen, chairman and president of International Telephone and Telegraph; Wayne C. Marks, former president of General Foods; C. R. Smith, president of American Airlines. Quite an array of names. They all started their business lives as accountants.

No doubt about it, accounting has been the fastest-growing profession in the country for a long time. There are close to 100,000 CPAs in the United States today, plus another 350,000 noncertified accountants. The big public accounting firms in New York are so desperate for talent they are turning to hitherto ignored sources, such as City College. Some are even hiring girls. Firms such as Peat, Marwick & Mitchell or Lybrand, Ross Bros. and Montgomery, two of the "big eight" that dominate the public accounting field, have as many as sixty partners operating in some 250 offices on six continents and in fifty nations. They are twice the size of the largest advertising agency, with ten to fifteen times more clients than the biggest Wall Street law firm.

A promising man in these firms is almost guaranteed a partnership, with an income in the $25,000 range by his early forties. If somehow he doesn't make it inside the firm, he stands a very good chance of moving out into the business community, where accountants, to hear the AICPA (American Institute of Certified Public Accountants) tell it, are viewed by businessmen as combination Einstein-Houdini's, with all the answers to a corporation's woes in their audit-trained eyes.

So goes the rosy side of the picture. But there are some darker shades. While numbers of men with accounting training undoubtedly do go to the top, a great number of others have been persuaded by the propaganda to believe they have the stuff when they obviously don't. A discouraging percentage of letters from frustrated executives, that land on my desk each week, come from accountants.

In the past at least, the field has attracted a great many people who are good at working with figures but not especially talented at working with people. There is almost a fad among corporations for "financial vice-presidents." Recently a nonbusiness friend of mine asked me what they were exactly, and I said, "An accountant with a personality."

There is some truth as well as a little humor in that remark. Lately the big eight firms have become more and more disenchanted with business school graduates and have taken to hiring liberal arts men and giving them the accounting training they need. The result is a more rounded personality, a man who can not only audit books, but charm clients.

When I really want to make the college seniors sit up (or wake up) I give them my farthest-out-against-the-tide career, labor leader. That's what I said, *labor leader*.

I do not know of any area of American business that suffers from a greater shortage of executive talent than the labor movement. Nowhere is there a wider market for energetic young men with a genuine grasp of the techniques and practices of modern management.

At the moment the American labor movement is in a kind of twilight, a shadow period cast by the men who rose to power in the 1930s and 1940s and are now about as contemporary as a Packard sedan.

Already there is an almost monumental generation gap between labor chiefs and the rank and file. Many chiefs gasped with disbelief when their statisticians informed them not long ago that the majority of their membership is under the age of thirty. Anyone who associates with the older leaders for more than an hour will almost infallibly hear them grumble about the young folks' indifference to their tales of Depression days when unions were fighting for their right to exist.

For the moment these aging Turks are in control and so is their "hate the management" psychology. The antagonistic spirit which still erodes so much of labor-management relations in this country will, I predict, slowly vanish when the next generation takes charge. These young men will be labor executives whose proudest boast will be not the number of times they got arrested or beaten up on picket lines, but how well they can talk management's language. With more and more skilled workers earning over $10,000 a year, it simply doesn't make sense to picture management as a compound of Scrooge and Simon Legree. These young men will see that both sides can get far more out of our fantastic technology by cooperation.

I'm not suggesting that strikes and disputes will disappear entirely. No, the millennium will not appear overnight. But when you go down to Washington and look at the Teamsters' national headquarters, or out to Detroit and see the equally corporation-sized offices of the United Auto Workers, it doesn't take much imagination to understand what I mean when I say unions need executive know-how. They need it just to run their own affairs. A recent survey by the AF of L-CIO's Committee on Political Education (COPE) reported that most union members form their opinions on issues not from union publications but from television programs, newsmagazines, and newspapers that all of us see and read. This means that the rising tide of under-thirty members is not going to put up with the get-me-rich, slipshod policies with which too many unions have been run.

From two points of view, then, profit and self-preservation, unions are going to awaken very soon to a desperate shortage of executive talent. If you incline toward a career with an unpredictable future, Big-Time Unions, Inc., could be for you. Don't worry about having to sing "Solidarity Forever." Like any good executive, all you'll have to do is deliver the goods in the annual report.

I could go on enumerating hot careers until this book was bigger than an unabridged dictionary. But my point, as you have no doubt gathered from the chapter title, is the *style* of success. Everything I've said so far is aimed at convincing you of the importance and practicability of this style—moving with change and against the tide. But there is another aspect to style, which emanates not so much from choice as from personality. Whenever this topic comes up I think of Joe King.

I can still see Joe standing there in that big paneled

office, a cocky bantam in a $300 suit, coolly telling the executive vice-president in charge of sales that he didn't know what he was talking about. The VP outweighed Joe (which is not his real name, of course) by fifty pounds, and I thought for a moment I was about to become a witness to a murder. A district sales manager doesn't talk that way to a vice-president.

Back in my office, I made a note and dropped it in my file under K. It read: "Check Joe King in two years."

Two years to the day, thanks to an efficient secretary, I called back and asked for the sales vice-president. "Mr. King will be with you in a moment," said the honey-sweet voice on the other end of the telephone.

Joe King was a maverick. He always had a better way of doing everything, from sharpening pencils to setting up million-dollar deals. For a generation now the business world has been unable to make up its mind about this type of executive. Company presidents blow hot and cold from season to season. One year the mere mention of the word "maverick" makes them sit up and growl, "Get him." The next, they swear they would rather hire a two-headed idiot.

Through arctic and tropic weather the mavericks go their way. A great deal of their success depends not only on the general business climate, but on the local weather in a particular company. It so happened that Joe King at that time was working for a firm with a very flexible, open president. He liked new ideas and nobody in the company seemed to have very many except Joe. So Joe soared ahead and got delusions of grandeur.

He switched from his original company and tried trending up to a firm three times its size. They favored the conference and the committee approach and Joe very swiftly made himself persona non grata to almost every executive in the place. It's one thing to tell a man off in the privacy of his office. He may not like you for it, but he may, if he has some integrity, respect you. It's quite another matter to wreck another man's ideas while a half-dozen other executives watch the performance. Then Joe would top the act by making it clear that he thought even less of their ideas.

Joe lasted only eleven months in that job. He came to see me and I found him another slot in a company even bigger than the one that bounced him. But they understood mavericks and put them into jobs where they were less likely to clash with more standardized executives. Joe tackled special projects, directly under the supervision of the president. He did an absolutely brilliant job of unsnarling a snafu in a major sales region. He flopped trying to bring some order out of labor chaos in one of their key plants. He scored another bull's-eye setting up an overseas operation in Australia, where they loved him. The last time I saw the president, he told me, "Joe's batting about .750. Which is pretty good in my league."

Some business soothsayers solemnly warn the maverick to change his style and conform, or else. I have always thought this is a mistake, for two reasons. One, the maverick will be miserable trying to do it. Two, the maverick can survive if he knows he's a maverick and picks his jobs accordingly.

Right now the business mood has shifted strongly to the pro-maverick side. So crank up your idiosyncrasies, fellows, and come on strong.

Movement is as essential to a maverick as breathing. Perhaps I've got a little maverick blood in my own veins. I've always been an apostle of change. But I would be dishonest if I didn't admit that over the years I have come across situations that force me to eat enough of my words to spell humble pie at least. There are times when a man should stay in a job. Stay and stay and stay, especially when he has a reasonably good analysis of an industry and himself. Let's take Harry Ernest, a fellow who graduated about the middle of his class in college, fought in Korea, won no medals, married a typical American girl, and has four healthy, voracious children. Harry is an average Joe, not stupendously talented in any one direction. He majored in business at college and showed a special interest in accounting. His first job was with one of the biggest banks in Ohio and it looks as if it will be his last job. He has been there fifteen years now. Bad? Harry likes the work and the bank likes Harry. He's a digger, a plugger. He puts in twelve and thirteen hours a day. More important, the bank put him in charge of studying the potentialities for data processing equipment ten years ago and this put him on the crest of the whole new wave of using computers and other automatic machinery, which is revolutionizing the bank business. Sometimes Harry's wife gets restless and talks about better-paying jobs elsewhere. But I tell her she's crazy. If Harry sticks it out, he's going to be president of that bank. Harry agrees.

He's sized himself up. He knows he's not one of the century's whiz kids, but he also knows he has a solid grasp on his specialty and he knows he's in a business that places a tremendous premium on loyalty and stability. He's going to stay, and he's going to be president—and those are words I'm sure I won't have to eat.

On the other hand, let's take George Allen, a sales executive for one of our major drug companies, in charge of over-the-counter products. Riding high in a volatile, fast-changing business, George is one of those men who dreams of the stability that Harry Ernest possesses. He never stops to think, of course, that he is earning three times what Harry makes. Some part of the other fellow's grass always looks greener. So instead of translating stability into a concept that *includes* mobility, George takes the word literally and tries to build himself a little fortress inside his company. When sales slump, he uses the scapegoat technique. Assistants are crucified, the marketing vice-president is an idiot who creates impossible sales quotas, faithful yes-men are rewarded with nonproductive spear-carrying jobs. George may keep up this performance for two or three, maybe even five declining years, if he has a weak president who is sentimental about firing people. But the day of reckoning inevitably dawns. The president retires or moves on to a better job and the other executives form a let's-get-George-Allen club and march on the new chief executive. George is out on his ear without even a decent recommendation. If he had moved when he was riding high he could have taken with him a ton of admiring fan mail from his fellow executives.

51

Now he has nothing but a legacy of dislike and double-talk. George is on his way down, and probably out. The moral? There isn't any. Business is not a morality play. The pure in spirit are only rewarded if they use their heads as well as their hearts. And occasionally eat their own words.

MISTAKES AND HOW TO
UNMAKE THEM

How not to is one of my favorite subjects. It is awfully hard to make positive advice fit a specific individual's career. But career mistakes are so common, and so universal, that they can be pinpointed and discussed. Accentuating the negative may sound like a strange way to move up, but the successful man in modern business is not merely someone who does his job well. He avoids with equal skill a host of moods, moves, and mannerisms that can negate his achievements. As an example of what I mean, let me tell you the story of Joe Adams.

Joe was a marketing genius. Associates swore there was a miniaturized computer inside his head. He had a sixth sense for sniffing out soft territories, suggesting new products. He could point without boasting to a string of triumphs that made presidents palpitate and treasurers salivate. Yet

Joe never stayed long in one company. Turmoil, dissatisfaction, sometimes sheer chaos seemed to trail in his wake. Why?

Because Joe was a destroyer.

He had a failing all too common in high-powered executives. He simply could not tolerate weakness in people under him. The smallest lapse set his teeth on edge. Anything from a sloppy report to leaving coffee rings on a desk might bring on a tantrum. These days employees simply won't take that sort of treatment. The turnover in Joe's department was always disturbing to his fellow executives. Ultimately it would begin to interfere with the operation. Finally the president would decide that much as it paid to have Joe around, another man could do the job almost as well, with a lot less wear and tear on everybody's nerves.

I studied Joe's record carefully, and I knew all about his problem when I placed him as marketing director of a $300-million-company. I told him I was ready to give him my unqualified recommendation if he would agree to take one piece of advice from me.

"What's that?"

"I want you to set yourself up in an office where you have as little day-to-day, run-of-the-mill contact with the rest of the people in your department as possible. Make it impossible for you to watch them as they do their jobs. I don't mean you should become a hermit, of course, I just want you to concentrate on the purely executive problems and steer clear of the details."

Joe agreed. He has been with that company for five

very productive years. They have also been peaceful years. The president of the company cannot understand why Joe didn't get along with the personnel in his earlier jobs.

Joe himself is a little amazed by how simple the solution has been. I saw him the other day and he offered me some philosophic thoughts that are worth passing along.

"I realize now you can't expect more than 20 percent of your staff to be producers. You've got to be satisfied with the other 80 percent if they just stay even with the board. A man just wears himself out trying to change them for the better."

As a destroyer, Joe was a fairly average case. I've seen some far more terrifying examples, who required more drastic cures. At the request of the stockholders, one company president moved to an office twelve miles away from the mill because he was driving himself and everyone else crazy with his insistence on controlling and supervising every detail of the business.

It may sound strange, but walling off a destroyer is the ideal solution. It's sort of like surrounding an atomic generator with a lead shield. You get the tremendous energy without the destructive by-products.

With destroyers, we are discussing fundamental personality patterns. But a personal problem does not always have to be so broad. Recently Dr. Frederick F. Gaudet, for many years director of the psychological laboratory at the Stevens Institute of Technology, told me the story of a man named Stoneman. He arrived at the laboratory with a note from his company, Dr. Gaudet says, "that was one of the most heartbreaking things I have ever read in my thirty years as an industrial psychologist. It said, 'Is this man salvageable in any way?' "

Stoneman was a middle-level executive who had been with the company about a dozen years. The executives in the ranks above him were baffled by his failure to fit into the corporate team. He was intelligent, a thoroughly trained engineer. But no one would work with him. Report after report called him "uncooperative, unresponsive, a dead weight."

Dr. Gaudet and his assistants at the Stevens Laboratory of Psychological Sciences agreed to make a stab at salvaging Stoneman. He himself took readily to the process. After about a week of therapy—which consisted largely of talking about his problems on the job and his attitude toward his work—he said, "You know, I think the company must have sent me here because I'm in line for a promotion."

"Why do you think that?" asked Dr. Gaudet.

"Because when I walk around the plant, I notice that a lot of the brass smile at me now."

The following day the executive vice-president called Dr. Gaudet and in an awed tone asked, "What have you done to Stoneman?"

"Nothing but let him talk," Dr. Gaudet said.

"It's unbelievable," the executive said, "Now when you smile at Stoneman—*he smiles back.*"

Smiling back was the beginning of Stoneman's resurrection. He is now an upper-level executive with that same company, and is rated one of its most valuable leaders. His story is by no means the only proof that small details of personality which most men rarely stop to consider can spell the difference between success and failure. Dr. Gaudet tells of another man, a tall, confident six-footer with a booming voice. He was a research chemist for a drug company, and had done brilliant work as a scientist. But when he moved into an executive position, man after man quit rather than work for him. The company was close to firing him as hopeless when they sent him to Gaudet. Only when he reviewed his conduct in detail did he realize that he habitually spoke to his assistants in a loud, exuberant way, which many men found overbearing and obnoxious.

Still another man, a troubleshooter for a construction company with a brilliant record, suddenly went sour. He began causing more problems than he solved, quarreling with subordinates and superiors over policy and becoming sullen over supposed slights. His company gave him a blunt alternative: consult a psychologist, or be fired.

He went to Dr. Gaudet, and gradually he came to see that he was taking out on his fellow employees his resentment against a domineering wife. He had been married to the woman for twenty-five years, but while their children were growing up she had been too busy running their lives to torment him. Now they were grown, and she had turned her full attention to him. He disliked it—but he was only dimly aware of how it was affecting him emotionally until he talked with Dr. Gaudet.

Actually, when we analyze these small things a significant pattern emerges. Basically sound men (and women) become so wrapped up in their own problems that they lose their normal awareness. They no longer realize how they are affecting those around them. A special kind of self-centeredness explains much of these personal failures—which are particularly tragic because they are unnecessary. Experts say that ten out of every eleven failures in business can be traced to personality. They rarely tell us how often these failures are minor quirks or temporary emotional phases. All most men need to eliminate these mental blemishes is a little more self-awareness.

Sometimes the problem can be outside rather than inside a man—how he looks. A few years ago I sent a prospect to Boston to be interviewed for a top job with a $500-million-company. I had interviewed the man at his home, relaxing on his patio in a sport shirt and slacks. He had convinced me he was perfect for the job and I was stunned when the company curtly refused him. Talking it over with the president, trying to find out why, was even more frustrating. The president couldn't really explain why he had turned him down. Then I noticed that the president kept saying, "He just didn't look right."

Back in New York, I took the man to lunch and saw at a glance what was wrong. He had lousy taste in clothes. His suit was a cheap cut, his shirt didn't match his tie, his shoes were unshined and shabby. I took him to one of the best clothiers in town, restyled him from his hat to his socks, and sent him back to Boston. This time the president hired him.

Neither the top men who do the hiring and promoting nor the people who are trying to fight their way into the corporate suites give sufficient thought to why they hire or promote Joe X and pass over Jim Y and don't even look at Jack Z.

A very bright lady named Garda Bowman has done a remarkable Ph.D. thesis at New York University—"The Image of the Promotable Person." Studying both local New York firms and national firms, she found overwhelming evidence that most promotions were made on the basis of an image of the typical company executive. If this image does not include men with Italian names, short or fat men, flashy dressers or mustache wearers, the chances are all too good (or bad) that people in these categories will not get the promotable nod.

In our fast-changing melting-pot society, the typical corporate image is all too often dated. As business commentator Jack Homer wrote recently: "Apparently the ideal type for company image building is vintage 1947 Van Johnson as shown on the 'Late Late Show.'"

More and more businessmen are starting to realize they simply can't afford to let this company image interfere with their substantial judgment of a man. The research director of a U.S.-based international food processing firm spent eight months searching for a rather rare specialist—an enzymologist. He finally succeeded in snatching one from a leading university. When he brought his prize catch in to meet his superior, a staff VP, all hell broke loose. In a hurried private conference the research director was told, "We can't hire this man. He has a moustache."

The research director demanded to know where and

when and by whom it was stipulated that the company banned moustaches. The VP stammered and stuttered and could only say it had "always been the policy."

"Well, I've got news for you," said the research director. "It isn't any longer."

The moustached enzymologist got the job and has proved to be an invaluable addition to the research staff.

The story is a perfect illustration of how the promotable image usually operates—on an irrational, subconscious level. Most of the time when they are looked at with a reasonable, critical eye, the taboos are pretty silly. But they are hard to buck and anyone who is launching a corporate career should take a long, hard look at a company's executives and check out the overall image against his personal image. If he is five foot eight and every vice-president is over six feet, he may be in for trouble.

Of course, he can still get in the race, hoping that by the time he is ready for a top job the company's promotable image will be more in touch with reality. Personally I am firmly committed to the idea that no company can afford to overlook talent these days, no matter how it is packaged. But alas, they do, and for the time being the smart man will live with this fact.

Now let's widen the circle a little, moving out from the individual man to his personal relations. Let's begin with the closest and most personal relation of all, his wife.

Last year I had an opportunity to place a New York executive with a top Midwest company. He was sick of New York's traffic and high taxes. Moreover, there was a substantial raise involved. As a final (and what I thought a routine) precaution before recommending him, I called his wife when I knew he was out of town and asked her how she felt about the move.

"Well," she said, "it's going to be quite an uprooting. I mean the children changing schools after five years, leaving friends. They're terribly upset. And my mother and father have an apartment in this building and they're upset too. They'll never get to see us now. I'm going to miss my mother, I mean I practically *lived* in her apartment when Harry was out of town. But if this is what Harry wants, I'm not going to stand in his way."

Harry did not get the job. I did not recommend him.

I knew from harsh past experience that when an executive moves, a martyred wife is ten times more destructive than the woman who flatly says she hates the idea but is prepared to go along because, after all, she is married to the guy.

Some people have criticized business for trying to size up a man's wife before they hire him. People like Vance Packard have denounced this as an invasion of privacy. But no company president I know is interested in studying a potential executive's wife for any reason but one: self-protection. Business doesn't want to invade a man's private life; in fact, "invasion" is really an exaggeration of the highly discreet investigation on which most appraisals rest. But top executives have found time and time again that a dissatisfied wife can wreak havoc on a man's job performance.

In a small company town, an out-of-sorts female can

wreak even more havoc, starting uncalled-for feuds between herself and other executive wives, which soon spread to the executives themselves.

At the same time, I sympathize with the women who find themselves caught up in the executive checkers game which so many companies seem to play to the point of near madness. It isn't at all uncommon for a young executive in a big company to move six times in eight years.

Some companies are taking long, hard looks at this policy, which was supposed to give a young comer maximum experience in all parts of the country before he settled into the main office. More and more the procedure begins to look like some sort of ritual torture, which the young couple must go through to win their credentials in the executive club.

But in spite of these signs of hope, moving remains a basic problem for the executive and his wife. It is something they should not dodge. They ought to thrash it out, even if it involves some yelling and screaming. It is absolutely essential for both man and wife to know how each feels about the move.

Nothing is more fatal to a man's career than a botched move. The company he abandons is infuriated over the money it has spent to move him, not to mention the gap they must suddenly fill. When he comes shambling back to where he started, his business friends are bound to snicker about "poor old henpecked Harry."

That is why the martyred wife who disguises her real feelings and pretends she is ready to make the sacrifice is the biggest menace in a moving situation. Harry didn't know it, but I was doing him a favor when I refused to recommend him for that job.

Recently I was confronted by what was to me a new type of marital woe. It arrived in the person of a young man who was so wet behind the ears he got water all over my carpet. He also ran off at the mouth in an almost frantic manner, insisting that he had to get a job in the $20,000 range immediately.

He was the son of a good friend and all of twenty-six years old. I patiently explained to him that he simply didn't have the experience to make this kind of money in his field, which was heavy industry. Another ten years maybe and—

"Another ten years and I'll be hiding out from every loan shark in town."

I calmed him down enough to get him to tell me his story. He and his wife, armed with college degrees, had both worked for the first five years of their marriage. They'd both done rather well, she in advertising, and soon they were pleasantly amazed to find themselves living on close to $20,000 a year. Then came the day when his wife decided it was time for them to have a family. Unthinkingly he agreed. Only now, when she was thoroughly pregnant, did it occur to him that they were about to lose her $8,000 a year and that somewhere, somehow either it had to be replaced, or an austerity program had to be inflicted on their budget that would make even an Englishman wince.

Amazed to find myself sounding like Harold Wilson, I told him to choose austerity for the time being. Much as I am inclined to favor young men in a hurry (I was one myself), I am wise enough now to know that hurry of the frantic variety can drive a young man into job choices that cheapen rather than deepen his career. There are companies that will pay more money for a young man, but they usually have unsavory reputations, and the job span of their executives is too often brief and bitter.

The man who jaws his way into responsibilities that he can't handle, and then falls on his face, has set himself back three years. The worst part of this syndrome, however, is the subtle erosion of the marriage itself. The young executive may not even be aware of it as first, but he is bound to resent this woman who is pushing him beyond his depth, forcing him to take risks that in his heart he knows are destructive. When failure strikes he may turn on her and wind up losing both his job and his wife.

The smartest young couple I know had that delicious sensation of two incomes for six years. But they did not spend a cent of the wife's salary. They put it all in the stock market and lived in reasonable comfort on the husband's salary. By the time the wife decided she wanted to start a family they had a $50,000 portfolio, which has since grown to over $100,000, and this cash reserve has given the husband a sense of independence and mobility which he has parlayed twice into strikingly shrewd upward job changes. So don't put me down as an old fogy who thinks wives should not work. I am all for it. But what a couple does with that extra income can make the difference between a happy, thriving career and marriage and an uncertain, driven flirtation with disaster in both departments.

Second only to the wife when it comes to personal relationships, is the rapport between a man and his boss. If that goes sour, it pulls the plug on the whole success circuit. This is what happened to my good friend Pete Hammond. An English major at Michigan State, Pete had most of his business experience in sales. It was good experience. Pete was a good man. He took a job as vice-president in charge of troubleshooting for a shaky Midwestern farm equipment manufacturer. The president, with whom Pete had to sit in almost daily conferences, was an engineering graduate who had come up via the plant manager-manufacturing route. Within three months he and Pete were communicating by memo and Pete was looking for a new job.

What went wrong? Pete picked the wrong boss. Nothing is more crucial to success, especially in the upper levels of business, than this often neglected consideration. We have had so much verbiage thrown at us about abstract concepts of managing that too many people forget that sandwiched between the abstractions there is, and always will be in every job, a crucial human relationship. Like almost every problem in life it can be improved, if not totally solved, by giving it a little preliminary thought.

Almost no one seems to realize the importance of some *similarity* between himself and his boss. In the past this often had unpleasant ethnic or religious overtones, but more and more, as business becomes more professional, it is a similarity of *career* that is important. A man who has been successful utilizing the resources of his own educational and business background inevitably tends to have more confidence in the judgment of someone who has had a similar background, and this confidence can make the difference between successs and failure in an executive relationship.

A man who wants to move up should take a long, hard look at the boss before he joins a company. This is especially true in the small and medium-sized company, where the president's personality is likely to pervade the entire operation. If the big man started out as an accountant and spent most of his career in the paper industry, and you can't stand figures and barely know the difference between rag and toilet paper, watch out. If you are a country boy with a cow-college degree and he is New York City born and bred with an Ivy diploma on his wall, be even more dubious.

I know this doesn't sound completely fair, and most bosses, if asked a direct question about it, would protest that they bend over backward to make room for personnel differences. But by these they usually mean personality differences. All of us have learned enough psychology these days to know that we must adjust to different human types. Introverts must learn to work with extroverts and so forth. But this is basically a negative consideration. We have learned *not* to be hostile toward other people's differences, but unless we change human nature I fail to see how we are ever going to make drastically different people *simpatico*—and it is the *simpatico* experience that makes for promotion.

There are, of course, switches that can be played on this basic idea. I know one top executive, a very sophisticated city-bred, college-educated type, who hired as his right-hand man a country type who had never even gone to college and who was proud of his ignorance. "I feel he's got the common touch," the president told me. "He supplies something I lack." But when it came time for him to retire, he didn't nominate this corporate Snuffy Smith for the top spot. He picked an almost exact replica of himself.

You can't use similarity in any open way. It is something that should be carried in the back of every man's mind and used when *choosing* a job. After that, forget it and start working your head off. No matter how much the boss feels *simpatico* when he looks at you, the feeling won't last very long if you don't produce. But if you are willing to do the job, picking your boss with care can help guarantee that your hard work will pay off.

As important as similarity is the tricky matter of familiarity. One day not long ago I met an ambitious young salesman for a major steel company, the son of an old friend. He looked extraordinarily pleased with life, and I asked him why. "I just got into my boss's country club," he said, practically chortling with glee. "I've been on the waiting list for over a year."

"I hate to sound like a pontificating old mossback," I said, "but I'm not so sure that's good news."

"Why?" he said, prepared to tolerate some wind from the defunct generation. After all, I am practically old enough to be his big brother.

"One of my best friends tried that approach," I said. "He got himself into the club and cozied up to the boss so well, the next thing you know he was getting invited to intimate little dinners for six. But it turned out that the boss

67

was more interested in my friend's wife than in his career. Finally, after a particularly obvious pass, the wife slapped the boss in the face, and my friend started looking for a job."

"My boss is a gentleman," the young man replied.

"Most bosses are, but even gentlemen have some strange quirks. I remember another fellow, who could have beaten the boss's ears off spotting him a ten-stroke handicap. But he always arranged it so the boss just squeaked through to victory. One night he got a little drunk with a very competitive fellow employee, and mentioned it to him as a private joke. The competitor leaked the story to the boss, and that was the end of one man's dream of golfing his way to the top."

"I'll keep my mouth shut," my young friend assured me.

"Then there are bosses who lean over backward *not* to show favoritism to someone they know socially. They can do you more harm than good. Then there are the unavoidable problems. How do you decide who buys the drinks? The boss feels he should always reach for the check. You feel you ought to pay sometime, so one day you reach for a whopper—and grandly sign away a half week's salary. The boss thinks: 'He must have inherited wealth—or maybe he's just careless with money.' Either way, you haven't racked up any white points."

My young friend looked somewhat unhappy.

"Then there's the boss who simply doesn't *like* employees horning in on his private life. When he's at the club he doesn't want to see you coming toward him, to discuss how to cut the losses in the Des Moines sales district. Even if you keep your mouth shut, you remind him of this and a dozen other headaches at the office. In his mind, you could gradually become synonymous with nervous tension, even nausea."

"You know," said my young friend, "I've been invited to join another club. More people my own age. The initiation fee's only half as much too."

"You won't regret it," I said. "More and more executives are learning that it's smarter to keep their private and business lives separate."

Now I was really pontificating. He looked at his watch and declared an imminent appointment called. "By the way," he said as we parted, "who was that first guy? Who had so much trouble with the wife-chasing boss?"

"Your father," I said. "You ought to talk to him one of these days. Believe it or not, you might learn something."

Your boss is the one man in the world you cannot afford to have for an enemy. Long after you have left his supervisory eye he can wreak havoc on your career with a bad recommendation. These days the quickest way you can make an enemy out of your boss is to quit in a foolish, hasty, embarrassing, or contemptuous manner.

There are numerous reasons for quitting a job. Two of the most obvious are a better opportunity from another firm, or ominous signs that you are in danger of getting fired. It is the first reason that requires analysis. These days, particularly in large companies, considerable attention is paid to turnover. It costs money to train new people, and the boss who has an abnormal turnover in his department is costing the company money and may be called up on a deeper carpet to explain himself. Aside from company policy, when you quit a job you are in effect saying "I don't like it here" at worst, and at best declaring that your boss has failed to recognize the magical quality of your talents. You are giving him the headache of filling your job, going to the toil and trouble of worrying over an unknown quantity, and perhaps spending long hours training the newcomer as he trained you. In short, if you think about it, it becomes obvious that the boss will not be happy about your departure. Even if he was planning to fire you, he would rather have done it when your departure suited him, not you. This way, you are really firing him.

How to do it? You have to sell him on the idea. You have to sit down and tell him why you think you are not the right man for the job you are in. You have to convince him that your time and talents can be better utilized elsewhere. His evaluation of you may not match your own and you may learn something from a frank talk along that line. But eventually he will be inclined to accept your evaluation, which is, of course, a projection into the unknowable future. If you have done the job well, you have involved him in your decision, and he may even end up feeling positively paternal about your career. This feeling may produce at a very crucial moment in that unknowable future a glowing recommendation when you need it most.

It hardly needs to be added that along with this approach there should be a wholehearted spirit of cooperation, aimed at making your leave-taking as painless as possible for him. You make it clear that you will wait for a replacement to be found, perhaps you'll even spend some time helping to break in the new man. But the essential point is the selling job. You are still firing the boss. But you are treating him as a human being, not some economic abstraction. With any kind of luck, you will get the same treatment from him. When you get right down to it, it's a somewhat subtle application of the golden rule.

Far more common than the inept departure is the bad promotion. Accepting one of these lemons is the most common mistake in American business.

That's right, a bad promotion. I know it sounds like a contradiction in terms. But I would estimate that 25 percent of the promotions handed out each year are personal disasters.

There are hard questions every man should ask when a new job title is offered to him. Too often it is two thirds title and one third raise. Sometimes it is a raise, with a title that means, for all practical purposes, nothing.

The most important question to answer about a promotion is "why?" Is it the logical result of the work you have done? Or are you being promoted into another department because you have failed to get along with the people around you, and especially your boss? An awful lot of people in American business "fail forward" this way, and their success is very temporary.

Once a good friend took me to lunch to celebrate his elevation to a vice-presidency. But it was not with the company in which he had spent five years building up a public relations department into his private empire. "They thought I could be more effective with the agency that handles our account," he told me. "So I moved over there and naturally they made me a vice-president."

Six months later the company axed the agency, and one month after that my friend was out on the street looking for a job. Too late he saw that he had not been promoted, he had been fired.

The most crucial promotion is one that involves a fundamental change in a man's job style. Visit any engineering school in the country and you can collect sad stories by the dozen about engineers who tried to make the big move from the laboratory or the drawing board to the administrative level. Equally mournful are the tales of those who blithely attempt to move from staff to line jobs, buoyed by the assurance, too casually purveyed in our graduate schools, that managerial skills are something you can carry around in your head. This kind of move requires a man to sit down and ask himself what he really wants to do in life.

The most dangerous promotion is the really big one—the job title a man has dreamed of having on his door for twenty or thirty years. When he finally gets it there is often a terrible letdown. A number of psychiatrists have actually coined a phrase to describe the phenomenon—"success illness." Among the symptoms are, believe it or not, acute depression, sudden hypochondriac fears about health, and a panicky feeling that he will fail to measure up. The moral to be drawn from this "illness," the headshrinkers tell me, is roughly this: don't invest too much emotion in a single job. Life being essentially imperfect, it will never measure up to these idealistic daydreams. Result: the real thing creates more feelings of loss than gain, hence the depression. Also, if you invest too much time and energy in the pursuit of this one supposedly perfect job, when you finally get it there is a dismaying sense of life being over. Far better to regard every promotion, even the ones with the maximum titles on them, as stepping-stones to bigger and better challenges.

None of this means that promotion is or should be considered a bogey. Most promotions are worth accepting and celebrating. But it doesn't hurt to look at them with a cautionary eye. The rose-colored glasses approach can be fatal.

The big lure in most promotions is money. We all want more of it. A man's attitude toward this necessity is crucial. It causes more blunders in job choices than any other single factor. Time and again men come into my office in search of a job and the first thing they talk about when they sit down is salary. "I've given it a lot of thought," a man who had been comptroller of a medium-sized company told me last year. "I can't take a cent under $25,000. That's my absolute minimum."

I smiled patiently, looked him in the eye, and said, "I have absolutely no interest in what your minimum salary should be."

As usual, the man blinked, became excited, began telling me about his mortgage payments, his children in prep school and college.

Again I had to calm him down. "Don't worry, I'm not

going to offer you coolie wages, but I think it may well be to your advantage to take a substantial salary cut."

Astonishment! For a moment he looked like I had told him to sell his wife into white slavery. This is the standard reaction of most Americans when you suggest a salary cut. This utterly unrealistic and often ruinous attitude is most acute, ironically, at the extremes of the salary scale. I know young men who passed up fantastic opportunities because they would not take a $1500 pay cut. And I have known other men who have passed up the chance to make themselves a half million dollars because they could not bear to part with the prestige of an $80,000 salary.

My advice to career-minded men has always been precisely the opposite.

Always be prepared to take a salary cut, even a substantial one, if the opportunity justifies it.

Let's say you are in the middle and like most $10,000 to $15,000 a year men are living right up to the hilt of your salary. You cannot picture surviving with $1,000 or $2,000 less coming in next year. What to do? Borrow it from your father, your father-in-law, your friendly banker, cash in your insurance, cancel your vacation plans. There are a hundred ways to make up the difference if you really want to do it.

Why? Because you have a shot at that assistant sales manager's job in ABC Company under a boss who's only two years from retirement. Just enough time for you to get the experience and merit real consideration for his job, which pays $25,000 a year.

Unlikely? Don't kid yourself. I have helped aggressive,

wide-awake men make this kind of move hundreds of times. Last year I persuaded a designer who worked for a major corporation to resign a $75,000-a-year job and take $50,000 from another corporation, which was in serious trouble and desperately in need of his talents. Today this man is worth more than a half a million dollars. To get him, the troubled corporation offered him the juiciest stock option deal in its history. Its shaky financial situation did not permit it to meet his salary level. But who cares about salary when taxes start annihilating 50 percent of it once you pass the $30,000 mark?

Opportunity is the key word today, not salary. Opportunity to grow, to gain experience which can be translated into a leap up the salary ladder that might take the man who refuses the pay cut twenty years to achieve. These days the man who lets his ego get involved with his salary is trying to win the potato sack race with a full sack of potatoes around his feet. Eventually he is going to start wondering why everyone else is kangarooing along so far ahead of him.

The man who falls behind in the money race is prone to prove the old Barnum adage that a sucker is born every minute. All too often he will be trapped by the career systems we have discussed in the opening pages.

Men regularly show up in my office in search of jobs because one of these executive developers played on their dissatisfactions and titillated their imaginations with dreams of economic glory. Invariably I am forced to tell them the grim truth—the man who quits a job before he's got another one nailed down ought to have his head examined. This is especially true of an executive. The market value of an out-of-work executive automatically drops about 300 percent.

The phony salesmen of executive dreams are by no means the only menace in today's job market. Almost as dangerous is the company president who hires away talented men from other firms, picks their brains of all their creative ideas, and then callously discards them.

It is unpleasant to admit that there are some men in this country who think other people exist to be used by them. They apparently do not think twice about uprooting a man from a company where he is liked and respected, often moving him and his family halfway across the country, and then firing him six months later.

How can you protect yourself from such an experience? It is not as hard as you might think. Companies have reputations which aren't really too difficult to discover. Merely checking the career paterns of the chief executive officers can tell you a great deal. How long have they been with the company? Have they all come in from left field, so to speak, lacking what might be considered essentials of background or experience? If so, this is often a sign that the unscrupulous president is having trouble recruiting top men. How much money is he offering you? Does it sound almost wildly extravagant, double your present income plus a blizzard of stock options? These men often pay very well, but they don't plan to keep you around very long at those prices.

You can, on the other hand, assess yourself in terms of the situation. How would you react if after six months you found yourself looking for another job? Executives move around a lot these days, so there would be no special disgrace involved, and if this move involves a considerable step up the ladder for you, it might just conceivably be turned into an advantage. But only if you are tough enough to take the treatment and come out fresh and eager for another round. Again, this may be something on which you could use some good advice. A wise, perhaps older friend, an intelligent wife can be a big help here.

We all want to move up, we all want to get ahead, but the successful man combines ambition with a large dose of hardheaded realism.

Money is not the only thing that shoves a man into disastrous mistakes. There are psychological compulsions at work in all of us, which can get out of control with disastrous results. I see examples in my New York office all the time. They act like nerve cases. They twitch in the chair, chew their nails, rumple their hair, and talk with machine gun impatience. "I'll take less money," they tell me. "I don't care what the salary is, within reason. I just want to get out of that company!"

Each time I hear these words, I feel as frustrated as a coastguardsman who risks his safety and sanity trying to rescue a beached whale. You've read about those crazed leviathans who for some reason blunder into shallow water and when they are towed out to sea turn around and blunder right back to the beach again, as if they were determined to fulfill a gigantic death wish.

I decided to do something about one of these executive types—let's call him Jack—who was about to become a beached whale, corporate variety. He was big—sales vice-president of a $50-million-a-year corporation. He had spent eighteen years with this company, the prime of his executive life. Now, for no discernible reason, he suddenly wanted out. Out at any price, in the shortest possible time.

I knew exactly what was going to happen, if I permitted nature to take its course. He would find a job—or I, with a little luck, might help him find one—with a smaller, hungrier company that simply did not match his class. He would spend about eighteen months there, and then he would appear in my office again, pleading for another transfer. Without the slightest sense of incongruity (beached whales apparently suffer from total memory loss) he would tear apart his new company, basing all his criticisms on their failure to do things the way they did them back in good old XYZ Corporation. He would change jobs again, and within a year repeat the ritual. From there the gyrations in his downward spiral would become smaller and smaller, until he vanished into economic and perhaps physical oblivion.

I see too many of these men in my office each year. I hear too many stories about them in my travels around the country. Baffled presidents ask me, "What did we do wrong? Why did Jack bug out on us?"

I went to see some psychologists to find out if they might have an answer. They cautioned me that every case had to be judged on individual merits, but said there were some generalizations that every executive ought to consider. After about eighteen or twenty years in a company, every man carries inside him an inevitable amount of frustration. There were suggestions that were passed over, promotions that seemed to be based more on favoritism than on merit; there are the minor quirks of one's fellow executives, which after several years become like the Chinese water torture. One psychologist told me, "I think these guys are going through the same emotional upheaval that prompts so many couples to get divorces after twenty or so years of marriage. In that group divorces have zoomed in the past decade." Another psychologist suggested I read *The Revolt of the Middle-Aged Man* by the late Dr. Edmund Bergler. It's a remarkably enlightening book, aimed mostly at preventing middle-age divorces. The parallel between the man who wants to dump his wife and the man who wants to dump his company is obvious from the first page to the last. Probably the chief frustration, in marriage and in jobs, is boredom. We can pinpoint the other frustrations, but boredom is subtle, it leaves you depressed, edgy, more exposed to the obvious frustrations and irritations.

What to do about it? I decided to be candid with Jack, and bluntly told him that he was a candidate for the beached-whale syndrome. Did he really want a job with more challenges, as he claimed? Was his president really such a walking collection of eccentricities and monstrosities? Had he talked to anyone about the practical aspects of changing jobs? When was the last time he'd taken a vacation? Maybe all he needed was six weeks off to tool around Europe, go hunting in northern Canada, paddle a canoe up the Amazon, whatever it was that he secretly wished he could do and (secretly again) felt that the job, those kids in college, the new mink for his wife was stopping him from doing.

The treatment worked with Jack, temporarily at least. He went home agreeing that maybe he ought to think things over before jumping. I don't know whether it will work permanently. The Coast Guard hasn't found any way to dissuade a beached whale once he becomes really determined to destroy himself. But then, you can't talk to a whale and they aren't very smart in the first place. You can talk to executives, and they are supposed to be the smartest guys around. I hope this book persuades some of them to keep swimming along in the sometimes murky corporate depths. In the long run, even though you can't always see where you're going, it's a lot safer than blundering around in the shallows.

There is one other even more damaging psychological malaise. Instead of the frenetic activity of the beached whale, it produces inertia. I call it mental retirement.

I will never forget a lunch I had with an executive whom I had long admired as one of the most dynamic and creative men in American business. He is currently vice-president in charge of operations for a $15-million-a-year company. Almost from the start of our meeting I sensed there was something wrong. My friend was not talking about business. Instead he spent a half hour telling me about a recent trip he made to Acapulco, where he had bought land for a retirement dream home. He talked about trips around the world, golfing in Bermuda—everything but business. Gradually I became aware of what had happened. My friend had signed a five-year contract with his new company—a contract that made it impossible for him to move but which guaranteed him a bonanza at the end of the five-year road. It did not take me long to realize that this contract had destroyed a good executive. Mentally my friend had already retired.

It happens all the time. The tendency to trade years of one's life for guaranteed security is the biggest blight in contemporary American business. The stock option which, properly used, can be the incentive an executive needs to drive ahead, too often becomes a kind of bondage, both real and psychological. Yet the executive who does not work with an eye for the optional deal, for capital gains cash, is equally in danger of becoming a salary drone with no real independence or mobility.

Mental retirement is a special threat to men in upper-middle management. Often these men have put twenty or twenty-five years into their career with one company. Unconsciously they begin to think that they deserved a *reward* for this faithful service. The vice-president's title on the door is not enough. They tend, instead, to concentrate on their right to four weeks' vacation, use of a company car, other prerequisites. They welcome the long-term contract—the longer the better. They forget that the only reward an executive can justly expect for his efforts is more—not less—responsibility.

The result is a contradiction in terms—living deadwood. A company can only handle so much of this commodity before it starts slipping. Finally a lumberjack type will take charge and do some murderous chopping. Glimmering go those dreams of retirement.

Nobody goes on strike when an executive gets fired. He—and he alone—must guarantee his own security. The best way to do it is by choosing jobs that challenge, stimulate, create. Where can you find them? In a company that is in trouble. That last word is, alas, too often enough to make many executives hastily retreat. Recently I conducted an extensive search for a team of young men who would be willing to move into a well-established but slipping company. I was amazed (and dismayed) by how many men turned down the chance.

To be in on the ground floor of such an event is an almost once-in-a-lifetime opportunity. A company in trouble is a company in search of leadership. It is almost always ready to reward handsomely the man or men who can give it that leadership. Sure, there is a possibility that even a good man can try and fail, but the executive who dislikes risks ought to get out of business and go into teaching or government.

Should an executive ask for a contract when he moves into a troubled company? Most of the time he won't get one, so don't bother to ask. Usually a man has about ninety days to convince the management that he can do the job. Even if he has managed to wheedle a one-year contract, it won't mean much, except financially. If he does not produce, he will be derricked into a do-nothing demotion and paid off anyway.

How long should it take to turn such a company around? Three years, five at the outside. If a man can do it, he can reap something that few executives achieve to-day—financial independence. A company in trouble is rarely able to pay a man in cash. They have to make the reward a really socko stock option deal. But the stock option is the only way that a man can achieve financial independence. In our high-tax era, salaries, no matter how high, are tread-mills along the edge of the abyss. I have put more than one man into these company-in-trouble situations and seen him emerge three years later a millionaire.

But I don't emphasize the financial reward as the first consideration, because it is never certain. More important for me are the emotional values. So often I hear executives complain that their best efforts go unappreciated. They are usually men who work for a big national corporation which has extremely high standards of performance. When a company breaks the world's record for profits, everybody in it is bound to be pretty good. To stand out you have to be something close to a superman. How different those executives would feel if they took their skills to a smaller, troubled company. Concepts, performances that are routine in the lofty realm of the supercharged corporate giant may seem almost miraculously brilliant in a more limited setting, especially when the performance may be staving off imminent disaster. I remember a man who made such a change coming to me a few months later to report ecstatically, "For the first time in my life I feel like a real individual." He was, I hardly need add, in no danger of mental retirement.

MYTHS THAT RUIN MEN

EVERYONE makes mistakes. They can be corrected by others or a man can correct them himself. As President Nixon has demonstrated, "comeback" is a favorite American word. I am far more troubled, when I look at business today, by *habits of mind* that are subtly destructive over a long period of time. Mistakes can disrupt a man's career. (It is like hitting ruts in a road.) But they rarely destroy it if he has a reasonable amount of guts and savvy. Myths are different. They do their destructive work silently, over long years, and often a man never wakes up to them as the deadly source of his unhappiness. At the top of this deadly list I put the failure myth.

I've seen this myth destroy too many men. One of the saddest cases was that of one of my old Marine Corps buddies, Bill Stanner.

Why did Bill fail? He never understood the nature of failure.

Double-talk? Not at all. Far too many people have a completely mythical image of failure in their minds. It is a compound of television and magazine cartoons, a synthetic drama in which the big boss calls them into his plush office and chews them out for ignoring a crucial order, or for milking the company till, or for fooling around with the female help. "You're fired," booms the boss, and down they go to their office, to clean out their desks and face the cold, cruel world.

This daydream version of failure is actually reassuring to anyone with half a brain. They tell themselves they are too smart to make any of these obvious mistakes. They are alert. They are on time. They do what they are told. They do not steal or otherwise ignore company policy. So they go on, blithely accepting their routine performances as the formula for guaranteed success.

They do not realize that failure in business has no resemblance to this myth. They do not realize that it is rarely dramatic, abrupt, definitive. No good executive fires a man for one mistake, unless it is an incredible whopper that endangers the very existence of the company. On the contrary, mistakes are often a sign of above average talent and energy, being misdirected because of inexperience. No, the reality of business failure can be summed up in a single word: gradual.

A man does not fail in five minutes. He fails in five, ten, fifteen years. His final failure is not a single gesture, but a tragic accumulation of a thousand omissions, evasions, and complacent excuses. American executives like to picture themselves as tough, hard-nosed. And in many situations they are. But when it comes to firing, they are the most softhearted people in the world. They are prepared to pay out endless miles of rope in the wishful hope that a man will stop hanging himself.

This was Bill Stanner's story. As a friend, I went to him five years ago and told him he was failing. I pointed out that he had been passed over twice when vice-presidencies were distributed. I offered to sit down with him and analyze his executive performance. But he politely brushed me aside. He was doing all right. No one was criticizing him. Sure, he didn't burn up the track as a sales manager, but did everybody have to be a world-beater? Maybe he wasn't the hardest worker in the world, but there were a lot of other people doing less.

Then came that grim day when Bill awoke to find himself the oldest sales manager in the company. And not long after, there was the regretful interview in the sales vice-president's office. The chairman had announced a new policy: youth was the order of the day. They didn't want aging sales managers. . . .

Nobody yelled. Nobody scorned him. If there was any emotion in his departure, it was pity. If he asked, "What did I do wrong?" they could honestly say, "Nothing, Bill." But in their silence would be the real answer: *you just didn't do enough things right.*

Almost as destructive is what I call the myth of non-success. If you are an average man, and most of us are, quite painful thoughts may occur to you rather early in life. You read or hear some know-it-all like Butler talking confidently about crashing the executive suite. But when you go to Standard & Poor's, or sit down with some campus recruiter and cast a cold eye on the organizational chart of a major corporation such as Continental Can, you cannot help noticing there is only one president, five executive vice-presidents, and nineteen or twenty vice-presidents overseeing some 48,000 other faceless toilers. Inevitably you ask yourself, "What chance have I got with those odds?"

This unspoken, usually unasked question is, in my opinion, driving more promising young people out of the business world than any other single factor. In brutal terms, what happens to the fallout? If you don't make that magic twenty-six-man presidential circle, are you condemned to a humdrum, meaningless job for the rest of your days?

The answer is no. To prove it, I went to Continental Can, which happens to have the executive statistics just mentioned, and asked them to lay all their management facts on the table. I even persuaded them to let me select some men who are, for the time being at least, on the fall-out side of a vice-presidency and ask them what they thought of their jobs.

On the numbers side alone, there are some pleasant surprises. There are 6200 men in Continental Can in some supervisory or managerial capacity. No less than 500 have the word "manager" in their titles. Most of the salaries are in the $20,000 to $30,000 range and a few are well beyond it.

Let's take Clint W. Eads, Jr., forty-one, a manager of a metal container plant in Cincinnati, Ohio. He has 400 men under him, supervises a branch plant in Worthington, Ohio, and is responsible for annual sales of $23 million. Does he like his job? Definitely. "Decentralization," he says, "has allowed me to make decisions and to achieve results. The company gives me a real freedom to operate. The fact that Continental has tripled its business in the past fifteen years has enabled me to grow with the company, from challenge to challenge."

Then there is Warren J. Hayford, the general marketing manager for Continental. A West Point graduate, Hayford is only thirty-nine. He went from salesman in the eastern metal division to his present position in ten fast-paced years. He sums up his job in two words: terrific opportunities. "The package industry," he says, "is growing, dynamic and changing so fast dullness is the last thing anyone worries about. There are no limiting factors restricting personal growth and development. What counts is your ability to perform and contribute."

Finally there is thirty-seven-year-old Donald J. Bainton, who came out of Continental's management training program and went from assistant foreman on an assembly line to general manager, production planning, metal, in the New York corporate office in exactly twelve years. What he likes most of all is the doublethink aspect of his present job. "You've got all sorts of decisions to make on a present or near term basis, and, at the same time, you have to draw heavily on your imagination for the long-range planning."

Dull, humdrum, meaningless, unrewarding? These men only stare at you blankly when you try to pin such absurd adjectives on their jobs. Nor is any one of them gnawing his guts away because he hasn't been made a vice-president. They are too busy—and too proud of what they are doing and accomplishing. If they are fallout, they are a very healthy, happy variety. In fact, they make the term itself ridiculous.

Closely allied to the fallout fallacy is the myth of top executive indifference. According to the cynics among our college professors and their recent graduates, the business world is an "establishment" where the only thing that counts is who you know. Whenever I hear this garbage, I think of a conversation I had with Bill Reed, chairman of the board of Simpson Timber Company. We were conferring on corporate development, and naturally we discussed gifted men in various key executive jobs with Simpson and its subsidiaries. As befits a good chief executive, Reed's appraisal of each man was sharply perceptive. Then he started talking about a young plant manager in one of his smaller subsidiaries. A real comer, he declared, and proceeded to tell me more about this young man than, perhaps, the junior executive knew about himself.

Here was the president of a major corporation who took the time and trouble to cast his appraising eye not just on his top brass, but six or seven levels down his corporate hierarchy to pick out a man who was showing above average drive and brains. Is this unusual? Absolutely not.

The good president today spends at least 25 percent of his time looking for talent, inside and outside his company. He devotes more hours to pondering plans for corporate development, in which the key factor is talent. He knows, from experience, that less than 15 percent of the next generation's executives will have that special dynamism that can convert plans into profits.

The average young person especially has no conception of how much emotion the top man has invested in his company. Usually he has played a vital role in building it over three or four decades. He wants this growth to continue. He has striven to be the best. He wants this striving to continue.

I am afraid the young see the top man only from the outside, a figure striding past them in the halls or occasionally sharing an elevator. Too often they imagine a totally wrong psychology for him. They picture him as smugly indifferent to the lower orders, enjoying his power and wealth, perhaps even murmuring, "After me, the deluge." They never dream of him looking at them and wondering: *"Can he fill my shoes twenty years from now?"*

It works the other way too. Not enough people realize just how much attention a president pays to failure. During my same talk with Bill Reed, I heard him note, with regret, the poor results a certain young man was getting in a distribution outlet 3,000 miles from the home office.

To those who know a little about life, there is nothing strange or remarkable about all this. It reminds me of a comment Omar Bradley made about his meetings with Eisenhower during World War II. "Whenever we got together," he said, "we talked personnel." In business as in war, the payoff is in the performance that bespeaks leadership and toughened talent. The failures are swiftly replaced, because somebody up there is watching, all the time.

Okay, you say, talent and hard work may pay off in

some companies, but what about the many firms where a family has its sticky hands on the corporate controls? Young people especially are often surprised when I fire back, "It doesn't make any difference."

In public, at least, nepotism is one of the least discussed topics in American business. Yet privately I constantly hear executives complain, "The boss and his family run the show. There is very little opportunity to get anywhere with the company." When the son runs the business, an equally common complaint is, "The son is not like the old man. He doesn't have the ability or drive. The only reason he can be president of the company is because he is the son of the owner."

This kind of thinking delights the cynics who believe that it is not what you know but who you know that counts in America. But in my twenty years of business experience I have dealt with hundreds of companies where nepotism existed. Yet I met only one case where nepotism held back company personnel, and I have seen only one instance where a son as president was not keeping the company up to the standards of others in the industry.

Few people are willing to acknowledge that it is natural for the owner of a firm to assist members of his family to progress to a higher income level whenever possible. It is only natural for a father to feel proud when his son, after years of education and training, steps into a key position where he hopefully will continue to build the company to greater and greater success.

Yet nepotism arouses such strong emotions that people

tend to forget it is perfectly natural. Most executives will concede that the owner is a highly intelligent person who with little or nothing at first has built up a sizable business through his own ability. Experience has shown that such men rarely allow personal relationships to interfere with good business principles and practices. As a matter of fact, I have found that most owner-fathers are harder on their sons and close relatives than they are on other people working for them.

Several times, sons of successful fathers have come to me for advice on whether they should take a job in their father's company or with another, "neutral" firm. I have usually advised them to go to the neutral firm, because I did not think they (or anyone else in their shoes) could stand up to the pressure their fathers would put on them.

Why does the son who takes over his father's firm so often succeed? It is fairly easy to explain. This second-generation man was in touch with this specific part of the business world long before the average outsider was exposed to it. Growing up he heard his father frequently discussing business problems and decisions. When he was older he was able to watch his father meet and solve other problems as well as handle personality conflicts between employees. In short, he learned almost by absorption hundreds of skills that the average manager needs a decade to acquire.

If a job is offered to you in a company managed by an owner or his son, consider it in the same light you would examine an offer from any other type of management. Ninety-nine times out of a hundred, you can be sure that nepotism will not stand in the way of ability and will not hinder your success.

The nepotism myth may scare men away from a good opportunity. But I am more concerned with myths that debilitate a man's spirit, that sap the drive he needs to move ahead. I saw one staring me in the face in a recent issue of the *Wall Street Journal*. The paper reported a study done by one Lee Stockford, a Cal Tech professor, who claims that 85 percent of the men aged thirty-four to forty-two in middle management are (or shortly will be) in a state of crisis. They blow up when a co-worker borrows a pencil from their desk. They browbeat their secretaries for "not anticipating improbable events" whatever that means. They go off in a huff when the boss does not immediately adopt their suggestions. Why—? Because they are unhappy to find themselves in operations that are "low on principle and high on expediency." This is a dirty way of saying that they don't like the way their company does business.

I frankly found this incredible nonsense. It simply had no relation to the realities of corporate life as I see them in my day-to-day contract with major companies. It did not even faintly apply to the thirty-four- to forty-two-year-old executives within my own organization.

To find out if I was seeing things at some sort of peculiar angle, I did a brief survey of my own. Charles D. Gadsden, vice-president of personnel for Indian Head, a national consortium with over fifty operating plants, said he was "amused at the thought" that 85 percent of his company's middle executives were unhappy. He said that the figure was wildly unrealistic for Indian Head, and the symptoms as described did not appear in his executives thirty-four to forty-two years old, but in the junior group, in their twenties. "We consider this kind of dissatisfaction a healthy sign," he said.

Allen Shusterman of M. Lowenstein & Sons, with 350 executives on their roster, simply snorted in contempt at Professor Stockford's claims. Dr. James Schmidt, a psychologist on the staff of Richardson-Merrell (Vick Chemical) was similarly unimpressed. "We do have a few men who run into the 'forty doldrums,' as I call them, but they are usually several years beyond forty-two," he said. Edward Palcot, vice-president for the Marine Midland Bank, says he never sees such symptoms except in the first and second years of employment—and like the Indian Head people, "we consider it a healthy sign."

Here are four knowledgeable men who flatly deny the validity of Professor Stockford's survey. Count me as a fifth. The survey is typical of so much academic writing on the business world. It is not only unrealistic, but it bears the imprint of subtle hostility toward practicing businessmen, which disturbs me even more. At a time when we hear repeated rumors of the difficulty of attracting our best young people into business, Professor Stockford announces that a business careeer practically guarantees them a nervous breakdown between the ages of thirty-four and forty-two.

Professor Stockford describes 2100 executives who are apparently so timid they prefer to stay mired in distasteful jobs and abuse their secretaries, rather than move. They may exist—I am not accusing the professor of making up his figures—but I flatly deny his claim that his 2100 cases represent a cross section of American executives. No middle manager worth his paycheck has to stay in a dull or demeaning job in these days of executive mobility.

As a management consultant and executive recruiter, I can personally testify to my profession's interest in supposedly dissatisfied men in this age bracket who are looking for new challenges. Last month a single company asked me to fill ten executives jobs with men from outside their organization. Close to 40 percent of all executive openings are being filled from the outside these days.

A man who stays in a nowhere job and broods over a boss who doesn't listen to him is not a typical American executive. I suspect, on the other hand, he is a typical college professor.

At the same time, realism forces me to admit that there has been a change in the *ease* with which promising young executives moved out and usually up, from one company to another, via the management consultant and executive recruiter route. Recently I met one of these fellow professionals, looking more discouraged than a hound dog in front of a cactus bush. I asked him how a man working in a growth industry could look so sad. "I've just been to three conventions," he groused. "I didn't find a single guy worth taking to lunch."

This experience is by no means unusual, nor are the cries of pain I have heard from other executive recruiters about how tough companies are making it for them lately. A survey by the National Association of Executive Recruiters has revealed that seven out of ten men in the field agree that information about executives is "harder" or "much harder" to obtain than it was two years ago.

Quite simply, companies have become more sophisticated about protecting their executives from the recruiters' siren songs. Once it was standard procedure to send promising young executives—the comers—to business association meetings and industry conventions. Now they keep them home. The average recruiter used to be able to get all sorts of information about a company's executives from the telephone operator. Now these people are under orders to be as uncommunicative as a CIA operator, and in some companies the internal telephone directory has even been abolished. Other companies have forbidden their executives to enrich their biographies in Who's Who in Commerce and Industry lest they sound too appealing to the recruiter's probing eye.

This operation has, by and large, been conducted with great subtlety and a minimum of fanfare. Many younger executives do not even realize it is happening. But it has deep significance for their futures. From now on, it is going to be more and more up to the individual to make himself visible to the recruiters. There is no question here of abolishing executive recruiting. It couldn't be done, even if the 500 top companies launched a national conspiracy. Management consulting and executive recruiting will continue to fill almost 50 percent of the top jobs in the country, because it has proven itself to be the cheapest, most efficient and effective way of filling these jobs. But the young executive can no longer sit back and expect the recruiter to find him as an inevitable result of his achievements.

How to go about it? Very early in his career he should begin to circulate his résumé to a carefully selected group of executive recruiters. There are over 500 of these firms in the nation, but only a relative handful are large enough to make the submission of a résumé worthwhile. The smart young man will not wait until he finds himself in a dead-end situation, or about to be squeezed out by a merger, or afflicted by a terrific itch to move, before beginning this circulation. It will be far better for him if he gets himself into what some companies call "the bright young guy file" early in the game. Even if a man does not have the slightest desire or reason to move, it does him no harm to receive an offer now and then. It builds the ego and it also enables him to maintain a perspective on his progress within his own company.

Eventually he will want to move. The executive who spends his entire career inside a single company these days becomes less effective for doing so. Moving is challenge, and challenge is growth. But from now on the first and most important move will have to come from the man who wants these things enough to reach out for them.

On the other hand, I am often disturbed by the number of men I see quitting jobs for trivial reasons. Whenever I hear of a young man restlessly switching from job to job, I think of my friend Bill Talbot. He succumbed to one of the most common executive myths: a man must *love* his work.

The trouble started with Bill's wife Helen. On the way home from a party celebrating the promotion of a neighbor, she sulkily asked her husband, "When are you going to get that big promotion? Never, as long as you're in a job you *hate*."

Something clicked in Bill Talbot's slightly liquefied brain. "She's right," he muttered to himself. "I just don't like selling."

Thanks to an influential uncle, Bill switched to an executive desk in a large department store. In six months he was griping about boredom and bureaucracy a lot louder than he had ever wailed about the tensions and discouragements of the salesman's life.

Bill Talbot had succumbed to one of the most common and least discussed temptations in modern America—blaming your unhappiness on your job. Thanks in part to Dale Carnegie and the other salesmen of success, and in part to romances of the business world such as *The Man in the Gray Flannel Suit*, the notion has been largely accepted that the man who is not brimming with enthusiasm every time he thinks about his work will never be happy, and even worse, never successful.

Of course it helps if a man loves his work. But, as Dr. Frederick J. Gaudet asks, "What do you mean by love? If we are talking about the all-consuming passion a man may feel for a beautiful woman, men who become this absorbed in their work are very rare. Moreover, we often find them to be far from the most stable individuals."

One psychologist studied a large group of people from six different levels of society—professional men, salesmen, white-collar workers, skilled factory workers, semiskilled workers, and unskilled workers. He asked them which was the most important value in their job. Almost invariably the professional man checked "opportunity for advancement." At the opposite end of the scale, the unskilled worker was just as consistent in checking "security."

Another study, of Harvard men entering a wide variety of professions, found that relatively few chose their careers because they found something especially attractive about the job. Most felt "destiny," in the form of a father or an influential teacher, had far more to do with their job choices. My own experience has led me to conclude that most people choose their life's work through a series of accidents and necessities, such as the need for hard cash. Interest—much less love—seldom has anything to do with it.

There are, of course, some situations in which a man's dislike or lack of interest in his work can cause him serious difficulties. A man who is not particularly interested in other people can come to loathe a sales job—and will almost certainly fail at it. Similarly a born salesman can take to drink if he finds himself at an accountant's desk. But these personal and psychological factors will usually come through as very strong emotions, of the storm signal variety, and a man will seldom have much trouble recognizing them.

In the long run there is a lot more to living with a job than loving it. There are some things about every job that drive a man crazy, and others that he likes. The mature individual learns to take some bad with the good.

What else has pushed a man into an imprudent move? Believe it or not, a big reason has been loyalty. It is one of the modern businessman's favorite words—and most dangerous myths.

I don't think anyone really knows what it means.

In the recent past, the word usually meant company loyalty. But this notion has become more and more confused in an economy where executives change jobs as often as three times in a ten-year period. On both sides, company loyalty has tended to dwindle like an icicle in April. Now a company is loyal to a losing executive for about ninety days. Then they call in their executive recruiter, who more often than not is on a retainer basis. The executive's loyalty to the company extends not much further than his stock option.

Lately loyalty has taken on personal overtones. Corporate teams are loyal to a creative leader, and often they move from one company to another en masse. This is the only significant loyalty in the business world today. But even here there is a lot of misunderstanding about how it works.

Some people seem to confuse loyalty with love. There is no doubt that subordinates will talk fondly of "Old Joe" and his amazing capacity for hard work and instant decision making. But is this the same sort of feeling a man has for his father, mother, wife, or children?

Recently a good friend became president of a company, replacing an "Old Joe" who was supposedly loved (and a little feared) by everyone from the executive VP to the office boy. My friend was so intimidated by all this evidence of affection for his predecessor that he decided his number one job as president was to win unto himself the same fervent loyalty the ranks had proffered "Old Joe."

Since Joe had been something of a nondelegator who made most of the decisions himself, my friend decided that the team would respond to a new era in which responsibility would be delegated to the nth degree. At first everyone reacted with vast enthusiasm. It was undoubtedly a heady experience for executives who had previously been given little or no chance to think for themselves. In fact, it was so heady it made a lot of them drunk with power, and they began riding off in all directions simultaneously like a bunch of Mack Sennett cops. The result was a lot of wasted energy —and money.

By the end of the year company profits had taken a nose dive—and so had my friend's popularity. Men who had been chortling over the new pleasures of independence and responsibility began complaining bitterly that too much was expected from them.

The moral is obvious. The root of loyalty is not what an executive gives his employees, whether the gift is responsibility or generous salaries. Men are loyal to someone who gives them a sense of security about the future—especially the security of their jobs. Damage that and you will find the loyalest of the loyal taking to the lifeboats.

Business loyalty isn't built around love. It is built around leadership. The heart of it is respect—the emotion of a professional for a fellow practitioner of a difficult and demanding art. Love is private. Loyalty is public. When the two get confused, everyone is in trouble.

There is one more myth that has affected a surprising number of young men: career by computer. There have been numerous stories in the business press recently about organizations that use computers to select job prospects. The implication always is that this is the wave of the future, and eventually everyone is going to have his destiny dictated by an impersonal indifferent machine.

Just take a typical new computer organization. It costs twenty-four dollars a year to belong. When you join you fill out a six-page questionnaire which asks hunch questions as well as standard queries for a basic physical, educational, and experiential profile. They then feed all these names and backgrounds onto a magnetic tape.

Companies sign up with this computer system for $450 a year. When they have a job opening, usually in the middle management area, they send the news to the organization, specifying the type of man they want. The organization cranks out of its computer the candidates who match and sends each a notification of the position opening. Three out of ten follow up, says the executive director.

A similar matching process for job searchers graduating from colleges and universities has begun operating recently. The company programs the student's major and minor fields of study, his grades, his college boards score, his extracurricular activities, and his military status, among other things. Then it runs them off against the needs of company recruiters and forwards to the employer the names and addresses of students who qualify. Charge to the company, $300; to the student, $6.

These outfits are by no means the only ones using computers to put jobs and men together. A number of top-level executive recruiters use them too. I use one in my own company. This inevitably brings up the specter of a 1984, technological society in which machines, not men, decide everything, including a man's economic destiny.

A glimpse of this kind of thinking was recently visible on Broadway in the play *Generation*. The nonconformist, beatnik-type character who drove the square executive (played by Henry Fonda) slightly buggy at one point broke into a song which ran as follows:

> I put my IBM card
> In that old pianola
> And it played out my whole life's song.

Artists love to scare the pants off us with these kinds of visions. But the accuracy of such a prediction is about as good as the science in such nuclear thrillers as *On the Beach* and *Fail-Safe*. No matter how many computers eventually get into the job-finding business, I can guarantee you that they will never select a specific individual for a specific job.

Basically computers save a great deal of time and effort in the preliminary search stage of finding the right man. I like to describe them as telling us "who's in the ball park." But they don't tell us much about whether Henry Adams can play right field or John Paul Jones is the right pick for shortstop. That kind of decision takes a combination of intuition and experience, which no computer will ever acquire. Even more important is that intangible but very special meeting of mind and emotion which can only occur between human beings. You may have all the qualifications that can be listed in a computer, from one to 1 million, to prove that you are the right man for a certain job. But when you go in to see your prospective boss, if that mysterious sense of rightness doesn't occur in the interview, if somehow you don't reach him, the chances are you won't get the job. On the other hand, a man whose qualifications barely run from one to fifty on the computer side can walk away with the good job simply because he has clicked with the man on top.

So don't lie awake nights wondering if someday you will miss your big chance because they spelled your name wrong when they fed it into the computer. Your ability and those other intangibles, your competitive spirit and drive, will continue to be decisive factors in a man's career in 1984 —and in 2084.

TESTS BIG AND LITTLE

ONE set of myths needs a chapter unto itself to unravel. These are the rumors—and a few truths—clustered around psychological testing. Almost everyone who goes job hunting these days will wind up taking a psychological test. Every sophisticated and ambitious man should thoroughly understand these highly controversial tools, which are worshiped by some personnel men and condemned by others. According to surveys conducted by such organs as *American Business* and *Fortune*, between 50 and 60 percent of all U.S. firms now use psychological tests in helping them determine who gets hired, promoted, and fired. A single testing firm, Activity Vector Analysis of Providence, R.I., assays over 300,000 workers and executives in a single year. Another leading firm, Science Research Associates of Chicago, boasts no less than 11,000 companies on its roster of clients.

For all the uproar within the industry, most Americans

remain blithely ignorant of what, exactly, a psychological test is, and how one is created. Most psychologists divide testing into four broad fields. First, and probably most familiar, is intelligence testing, used largely in education. Next is achievement testing, by which a person's knowledge of a particular field is measured. Civil service tests fall into this category, as do college boards. Next is aptitude or interest testing, by which a person's potential for a given job is measured. Finally comes personality testing, which analyzes and estimates a person's emotional makeup. Most of the argument revolves around the last two types of tests, which have been adapted wholesale by individual psychologists and testing companies working for American industry. The dispute is especially fierce in the realm of personality testing, which claims to be able to select people who will react positively to a job. Thus the psychological tester will analyze, say, the emotional requirements of a men's clothing salesman. The ideal traits for a man in such a job, he will decide, are self-confidence, extroversion, and sociability. He will then give prospects a test or series of tests designed to reveal the presence or absence of these traits. On the negative side, he will also attempt to screen out the emotionally unfit—the neurotics.

For instance, the very popular Minnesota Multiphasic Personality Inventory tests a person for a number of neurotic tendencies. To find out if a man is easily depressed, he is asked to affirm or deny such statements about himself as:

I am easily awakened by noise.

Everything is turning out just like the prophets of the Bible said it would.

A yes to both these statements indicates a depressive trend. To find out if the person tends to solve personal problems by developing physical symptoms such as cramps or gastric or intestinal upsets, the MMPI has a "hysteria" scale.

I am likely not to speak to people until they speak to me.

I get mad easily and then get over it soon.

Yes to both these statements intimates you are the ulcer-prone type.

The Bernreuter Personality Inventory is even more popular than the MMPI among the testers. In a single year Stanford University Press, one of several distributors, sold over 1 million copies. Here are some of the questions it uses to probe for neuroses:

Do you daydream frequently?

Do you prefer to associate with people who are younger than you?

Are you troubled with the idea that people on the street are watching you?

Have books been more entertaining to you than companions?

Do you usually prefer spending an evening alone?

Yes to these questions darkens your chances of landing that salesman's job.

Whence comes the tester's confidence that the answers to these questions are significant? He has faith that the norm —the original group from which the test is constructed—has universal or at least reasonably general characteristics. The MMPI, for instance, was constructed from responses to batteries of questions given to 800 clinically classified mental patients at the University of Minnesota hospital. Their answers were compared to those of 700 normal visitors to the hospital. Thus the hysteria-prone patients answered yes to the questions (and many others) noted above, and a majority of the normal persons answered no.

Other personality tests are constructed by taking a group, such as a fraternity, and having them rate each other for traits such as dominance and sociability. How these rated individuals answer their questions becomes the norm for these traits.

Gathering this basic evidence is, of course, only the first step in creating an acceptable test. Thereafter the test must be given to many other groups to tests its reliability and validity. Reliability means that the same group will get more or less similar scores if they take the test more than once. Validity means that the set of questions really does what it claims—separates would-be neurotics from normals, dominant or sociable types from weak-kneed recluses.

Validity is, of course, the crux of many of the arguments about testing. High on the list of problems is what is being tested. Not even the best psychiatrists agree on what constitutes a neurotic trend. Traits such as dominance, sociability, alienation, introversion, and extroversion mean radically different things to different people.

There is another, even more controversial branch of personality testing—the projective tests. Unlike the quizzes, which simply ask you to circle or check answers on a piece of paper, the projectors theorize that a man reveals his personality when he performs a task. For instance, he may be challenged to see ideas, images, feelings in such things as inkblots—the Rorschach Test. Also popular is the Thematic Apperception Test, in which the person is asked to construct an explanation from a series of drawings, all rather vague and indefinite, of two human figures in a variety of situations.

One TAT picture shows a young woman staring straight ahead, while behind her a much older woman rests her chin in her hand and seems to be musing over the girl. Here is how one person interpreted the scene:

> The young girl wants to go out on her own and lead a good life but this old woman wants to control her and make her do things as the old woman wants them done. Some of the things the old woman has told the girl were bad, but the girl had to do them anyway. She hates the old hag and gets tired of the control that the old woman has over her and kills the old hag. No one ever found out that the girl killed the woman so she is free to do what she wants.

From this response the tester sees a number of personality problems: unwillingness to assume responsibility for personal behavior, hostility, a tendency to solve problems in "socially unacceptable" ways. A man who gave such an answer would hardly win the tester's recommendation for the executive suite.

In the Rorschach, the man who uses the whole of the blot to see a form, such as a "crab's shell," is considered to be ambitious intellectually. If he sees a "high level of organization where it is not appropriate" he is suspected of striving beyond his mental ability. Breaking the blot into small, unusual details seems to be characteristic of compulsive people who want their response to exactly match the form they see. Some blots are colored, and if the person sees only the color, this is supposed to mean a lack of emotional control. Texture and shading responses are usually interpreted as indications of anxiety and feelings of inadequacy or depression.

How these tests are used varies widely with the company and the tester. The Klein Institute for Aptitude Testing uses several tests to compile a score for some thirty-three traits, which they combine to suit various jobs, as described for them by the companies they service. Klein and a number of other big testing companies, which rate people for as low as thirty-five dollars a head, rarely if ever see the subjects. Some companies let laymen, often in personnel, administer simpler tests. Activity Vector Analysis gives personnel men a three-week training course in administering their test, after which they are graduated as "Certified AVA Analysts." Still other companies prefer to send men to nearby university testing centers for a series of tests which may take two or three days and cost as much as $200.

The most ferocious critic of this diverse and complex business is Martin Gross, author of *The Brain Watchers*. Mr. Gross makes a sweeping indictment. As he sees it, "testing is neither scientifically nor morally justifiable. It is a result of our insane race to state everything statistically, our tendency to accept a methodology without critical analysis of its philosophy." Gross scoffs at the unreality of the traits erected by the personality quizzes, declaring they are aimed at the "square American." Salesmen are given Joe Miller jokes to see if they have a sense of humor; anyone with a hint of intellectual or imaginative tendencies is suspect. He points out that daydreaming was Einstein's favorite sport, yet to admit on the Bernreuter that you are a daydreamer is a serious error. He tells of one man who was denied a lucrative job working on defense base construction in the Arctic Circle because he had homosexual tendencies, according to the tester. The test's concept of masculine was "strictly Stone Age." Gross cites two competing testers, one of whom used personality quizzes to select salesmen who were well-adjusted, happy extroverts, the other of whom used projective tests to select salesmen who were supposedly alienated lone wolves in gray flannel, boiling with hidden hostility and an eruptive desire to succeed at any cost.

Almost as ferocious as Martin Gross in his critique is E. B. Weiss, columnist for *Advertising Age* and author of *The Vanishing Salesman*. To prove the gullibility of personnel men, the chief advocates of testing, he tells of an experiment conducted by Dr. Ross Stagner of Wayne State University on sixty-eight personnel men attending a conference. Stagner gave the men a standard personality test, and instead of the real results, handed them back a phony "Personality Analysis Report." It was composed of flattering generalizations taken from cheap astrology charts. Each man's report was identical, but his name was typed neatly at the top to maintain the illusion. Nine out of ten personnel men fell for the gag and praised the reports as "amazingly accurate" descriptions of their personalities.

What do the academic psychologists think of all this turmoil? A large number of them are seriously disturbed by the abuses of the testing concept in a business setting. By and large they deplore the tendency of testing firms to oversell their products with extravagant guarantees. Dr. John

Dollard of Yale University says wryly: "Tests do not always test what they are named for." He cited the Strong Vocational Interest Blank, which compares a subject's interests and prejudices to the attitudes of people already working in forty-five occupations. "If your attitudes coincide with the attitudes of the journalists on which the test was based, does this mean you should be a journalist? I would hate to rest a career on such a tenuous assumption."

"Generally speaking," Dr. Dollard says, "the more complex the job, the more difficult it is to construct a test for it. What makes a good doctor, for instance? Someone with a scientific bent? Or someone with a good personality? A man who is good with his hands? Or someone with a high degree of empathy? The fact is, any one of these people can be a good doctor. Hence it is practically impossible to construct a test to predict which of a group of premedical students should enter medical school."

Dr. Frederick J. Gaudet, retired head of the Stevens Institute Laboratory of Psychological Testing and one of the country's leading industrial psychologists, says that too many executives use tests to escape the responsibility of making their own decisions. He tells a striking story from recent experience. An executive assigned to train his company's salesmen asked Dr. Gaudet to prepare a new battery of tests to improve the selection process. The trouble, the man explained, began about six months after the new men arrived. Thereafter dropouts grew alarmingly. "It seems to me," Dr. Gaudet said, "the first thing you should do is make a morale study." The implication that there might be something wrong with the way the training program was administered instantly aroused the executive's hostility. "The trouble is the selection," he insisted. Gaudet, just as stubborn, refused the job. A few months later, the executive brought in a tester who did not even have a B.S. in psychology to administer a new set of selection tests.

Who defends testing for business? The director of employee relations for a Midwest beer maker is typical of the moderate position. "We find psychological testing to be a very effective device in our selection procedures for management and marketing personnel. We use such tests in conjunction with interviews to fill such positions. But tests are not an end in themselves, and are only part of the total evaluation of the individual. Too great a reliance on testing procedures can undermine the position of individual managers, who must, in the final analysis, be responsible for the selection and promotion of their own personnel."

Unfortunately many psychological testers, in their pitch to prospective clients, sell the exact opposite of this reasonable position. It is not uncommon for a testing firm to sign a contract with a company which prevents the business executives from hiring anyone not approved by the tester. The glib explanation for this policy: unless he has complete charge of the hiring and firing, he cannot guarantee to produce clear-cut results. Stories abound of testers who flatly and categorically tell an employer that a job prospect should not be hired. One public relations executive told me of a tester who advised them not to hire a newspaperman because he was "too intelligent" for public relations work and would be a disruptive force in the agency. "We let the man go, and he was soon burning up the track in another firm," the PR man said. "So we decided the tester wasn't intelligent enough—and fired him."

There is a radical difference between this kind of huckstering and psychological testing as it is conducted at such academically oriented places as the Stevens Institute psychological laboratory or New York University's Testing and Advisory Center. At NYU the average client takes at least eighteen tests. Dr. Wallace Gobetz, the Center's director, says they always insist on giving each man a complete series. "Often we get calls from companies who want us to give a man a 'fast look'—'just the basic tests.' We always refuse."

Moreover, the tests are only the beginning of the evaluation process. "It is the interpretation of the tests which is all-important to us," Dr. Gobetz says. "It hardly needs to be added that this crucial step can only be handled by a trained psychologist." Dr. Gobetz compares this approach to medical tests. "An electrocardiogram, a urinalysis, a thermometer reading all state test results. But their final meaning has to be put together by a trained clinician. Taken separately, or even together, by a layman, they mean nothing."

How various scores were achieved is equally important. Take the IQ. Perhaps a man scores 120. Did he do better on the verbal sections or the numerical sections? How did he react to the test itself? All these observations are very important. An extensive interview is also irreplaceable."

Dr. Gobetz has nothing but scorn for testers who evaluate job applicants on the basis of test results alone, without interviews. "It is like trying to make a medical diagnosis by telephone," he says. "It just cannot be done." The Center also insists on interpreting the test results to the client even when the man has been sent to them by a company. (Many other men come to university centers voluntarily, for vocational guidance.) "We insist on feedback," Dr. Gobetz says. "Testing can cause anxiety, and we feel it is part of our professional responsibility to help the man handle these feelings. Also, if there is anxiety, this should be considered in our final report. We try to give an objective picture of the whole man."

Dr. Gobetz showed me a sample of the closely typed two-page report which the Testing Center sends to a company when a man is tested. "We always make it clear," he says, "that the company must make the final decision on the man's suitability. We never, repeat never, recommend hiring or firing a man."

Again and again, Dr. Gobetz emphasized that tests are not infallible. "I know of no test that predicts with 100 percent accuracy. I know of no reputable test expert who ever made such a claim." Just how accurate are tests? "If tests are judiciously chosen, the results can materially improve personnel selection—they can improve a company's batting average. If, say, 50 percent of the salesmen hired turn out to be failures, with good test procedures this perhaps could be lowered to 30 percent."

The modesty of this claim is self-evident. If the hucksters of tests were as honest about their results, the uproar of criticism would quickly subside. True, with more honesty and stricter standards, psychological testing might also cease to be a $50-million-a-year business. But it is time for the testers to begin policing themselves before the government does it for them. No business which can radically alter so many lives can continue to ignore ethical and scientific standards. Dr. John Dollard of Yale sums up the growing uneasiness when he asks, "Should tests not known to be valid be prohibited as rigorously as drugs not known to be useful and harmless?"

Personally I always shudder at the government policing anything. I believe that a new generation of executives may well decide to police the testers before the government steps in. Meanwhile, individuals looking for jobs are going to be confronted with tests. Don't let them throw you. If you make a poor showing and don't land a job that seemed promising before you took the test, don't build a mental block against all tests. Try again tomorrow with another company. If a test is requested, take it willingly and then forget it. Even when a standard test is used, the results are likely to be as different as your mood or as the mood of yesterday's tester when he was giving you the test or preparing you to take it.

As Dr. Gobetz pointed out, one of the most important things to keep in mind when you are being considered for a position with a new company is whether or not your personality will dovetail with theirs. Some companies have engaged industrial psychologists to examine all the company's executives and "psych out" the characteristics that have played a major role in their success. A test is then designed accordingly and the answers that you give are compared with the overall answers given by the executives. In this way the company can get some idea as to whether your personality would fit in or clash. Obviously, if the answer is no, you don't fit, this is not a reflection on you. The American business world is very large, and there is room for many kinds of company personalities. On the other hand, if you feel a test is outrageously inquisitive in its questions about your sex life and other personal habits which have nothing whatsoever to do with your performance on the job, don't hesitate to use it in your overall analysis of the particular company and whether you should go to work for them.

TIME AND EMOTION

THE executive opened the door of his car and I climbed into the front seat. As I did so my eye wandered toward the back seat, and I saw enough flies, lures, rods, and assorted fishing tackle to open a sporting goods store. This man was responsible for selling $10 million worth of goods a year. I was out in Michigan trying to find out why the goods weren't selling. When he opened that car door, he gave me the answer.

He was a nine-to-five man. His real interest was in fishing. Over lunch, he couldn't get through the business discussion fast enough. Thereafter he talked about his plans for weekend and week-long fishing trips and the hours he spent practicing in a little trout pool he had built in his backyard.

He's got plenty of time to practice now. I called up his

boss in New York and put his name No. 1 on the "to be fired" list.

But the marketing man was by no means unique. Again and again, throughout this floundering company, I found that the men with managerial responsibility had succumbed to the five o'clock trots. They simply could not see why they should work any harder than their middle management people or the superintendents and the laborers in the work force. They didn't say this, of course. It was an assumption that ran through their thinking, and more important, through their work pattern. The result was sloppy decisions and inability to fire unproductive people or revise unprofitable production schedules. Symbolic of the attitude was the way management had built for itself a separate building a good half mile from the plant. Almost as if they were saying to the place that was producing their bread and butter, "Don't bug me."

I told this story to an audience of young college kids the other day and one of them stunned me by standing up and asking, "Why should the managers work harder?"

My first reaction was anger, but I quickly realized that this boy was only reflecting the attitude toward business of the so-called intellectuals who dominate our colleges. Moreover, I realized it doesn't do any of us any harm to get asked this kind of question. There is a tendency to trumpet the importance of hard work without explaining what kind of work. Here is how I answered him:

"You have to begin by assuming that you are a manager because you can think more clearly, more coherently, and make better decisions than the people working for you.

But it is not merely the quality of your thinking, it is also its quantity that counts. Assuming that you have salesmen who are thinking about their jobs from nine to five, you have to spend at least 20 percent more time thinking about these same jobs than they do if you are going to stay ahead of them.

"You are responsible for the performance of a group of men. This means you have to think about not just one job but many. You have to think about solving personal problems as well as business problems. You have to think about motivating the drone and channeling the hard charger.

"Above all, you are responsible for the performance of the men who are working for you. I don't use the word 'responsibility' in reference to fear. Of course, if they fail, your neck is in the noose. But genuine responsibility goes far beyond this simplistic idea. You are responsible for their jobs, on which their happiness and their families' happiness, may depend. You are not just a slave driver, you are a protector, a conservator. These men in a sense are entrusting their futures to you and you must not fail them.

"Those are a few of the reasons why an executive must work harder than the men under him. It is also why he looks for a capacity and willingness to work when he looks for executive material in the younger generation. The executive who loses this capacity is a sad shell of a man. Essentially he has lost his desire. He may try to fill his life with hobbies and leisure passions such as fishing, but the gambit rings hollow and eventually it takes only a word from a management consultant to blow him away. Not surprisingly, really, because he wasn't a real executive anymore. He was only a

Humpty-Dumpty shell, who rang hollow every time he opened his mouth. Yet I could feel sorry for him. He was the victim of a creeping malaise which is infecting too much of America, the vague idea that society—the most abused word in the moden intellectual's vocabulary—owes us a living. The five o'clock trots is a major symptom of the eruption of this cancer on the executive level."

Time is the crucial dimension in every executive's job. I am endlessly interested in ways to save it, and I am always giving advice to other men or seeking it from them on this all-important subject. One conviction that has emerged from my years of thought may be a little surprising. Most executives don't know how to manage their time. The other day I got a letter from a good friend on this subject, which sums up my thinking better than I could do it myself.

Dear Bill:

When we had lunch the other day I wasn't looking for advice as much as for consolation. I saw myself in rather tragic terms, as a basically good-natured guy caught between the irresistible force and the immovable object. I simply did not see how I could possibly give my wife and family the time I knew they wanted and needed from me—and stay in the race at the office.

I was skeptical, to say the least, when I heard you say that this vicious circle could be squared. This letter is my way of simultaneously eating a little humble pie and saying thanks for some very practical suggestions.

The first thing I did when I got back to the office was check my habits. Sure enough, I did find that I was consigning certain types of work to the take-home pile automatically. Any memo or committee report over a page in length was getting into this category. On the job, of course, it gives you a great feeling of freedom, but when I thought about it, I realized that this feeling led directly to a good deal of wasted time. You stretch a lunch that should take ninety minutes into two hours. What should be a ten-minute conference drifts into a forty-minute bull session. By getting tougher with the way I used my office time, I was able to reduce my take-home paperwork 50 percent in two weeks! And the net effect on the rest of the office was extremely positive. Nobody really saw all the junk I lugged home in the briefcase each night, but you could sense, even see, the way the whole office responded to the way I stepped up my work pace.

At least as important as this switch was your suggestion to consider the early morning rather than the late evening as a place to find extra hours. Nothing was doing more damage to my relationship with my wife than the three or four nights a week I'd call her and say, "Sorry, I'm working late." For her this meant dinner alone with toddlers for company, and she hated it. I've reduced this bad habit practically to the vanishing point by getting into the office at 7:30 A.M. instead of 8:30. With my mind fresh I get twice as much done in that extra hour as I did in the two after-five hours I was habitually taking. Now I miss a dinner only when a full-scale emergency erupts, and this does not bug my wife because I've taken your advice and done some homework on that front too.

We sat down and had a long, very frank talk about the number of hours I work, why I work so hard, and what I could do and she could do to make my needs and the family's needs mesh a little better. This led to some intelligent planning, particularly for weekends. We decided that I should keep a minimum of two weekends a month just about work-free, and on those weekends we should have a definite plan. A football game, a visit, a family picnic, a trip

to the zoo—it didn't really matter what we did, but it should
have some preparation and be a firm date. I found it amazingly easy to wrap my business needs *around* these dates.

On our free weekends my wife and I have a firm rule
that we will *not* go to business-oriented cocktail parties or
dinners. Too often, as my wife pointed out, these things
were nothing more than business meetings where the wives
sat in one corner talking about clothes and the children,
while the men hashed over problems they should have
settled in the office. These kind of bashes only increased my
wife's feeling that she was merely a convenience, a minor
prop, for my all-important career. Instead, on our open
weekends we have non-business friends in for dinner or go
out to a movie or the theater.

I'm still averaging a seventy-hour week. But now I'm
really enjoying it. Thanks for circling this square with a
new approach to an old problem.

Best,
Jim

Rethinking his schedule is by no means the only way
an executive can save time. We live in a technological
society, yet a surprising number of executives fail to appre-
ciate how electronic wizardry can save them precious minutes and hours.

A friend of mine, general manager of Record-O-Phone,
the largest manufacturer of automatic telephone answering
systems in the country, is a nut on this subject. His own
specialty is a good case in point. More and more companies,
he told me, are installing automatic telephones in the homes
of their executives. These days you never know when you
need a crucial decision or some information than can lead to

a crucial decision from a man who is working for you in New Jersey, while your headquarters are in Denver. He may be away for the weekend, visiting his son at college or gone for a Saturday on the links. The automatic phone he sells has a "telekey" which enables the owner to get any messages recorded for him simply by dialing his own number.

For the executive who disappears on week-long hunting trips to the upper reaches of Canada, or aboard a fishing boat off Key West, there is an even more sophisticated gadget, portable telephone outfit which works on micro-wave relay and enables you to call anyone anywhere in the world. You can sit on a beach, be in a ball park and still keep in touch with vital merger or labor negotiations.

The telephone in the car is better known. In fact, it has become something of a status symbol among the upper middle class. But in these days of massive traffic jams, it has practical as well as plonking value for everyone, from top executives to salesmen who travel between cities.

The wonders of miniaturization should not be ignored. There are telephones small enough to slip in a man's pocket, which he can carry while walking about a sprawling plant. If you need him, the pocket phone beeps, and he takes it out and talks to you directly at your desk. Also on the market are a number of mini tape recorders small enough to slip into a man's shirt pocket. More and more executives and salesmen are using them to record bright ideas and to rough out memos and reports on the run. I have seen at least one copier on the market for under a hundred dollars that is lighter than a portable typewriter. It can save the executive hours of typing or dictating time when he's on the road or working at home.

How often have you sat in your office until ten o'clock at night dictating to a machine, catching up on days of back mail, and then spent the next two days fuming because your secretary is glued to her transcriber, trying to catch up with you? You could have all those letters back on your desk the next morning if you used one of the many twenty-four-hours-a-day dictating services. Some executives deposit a permanent supply of their stationery with these services, so they are always ready to knock out that emergency series of letters to salesmen or customers that can put new momentum into a lagging campaign.

My favorite among my friend's list of time-savers is "Car Teach." Developed in Texas, it utilizes a small cassette tape recorder and a series of tape lectures on business as well as cultural subjects. An executive can broaden his mind, increase his expertise while in the car or stopping overnight at a hotel or motel. At the moment, the available Car Teach courses are a little on the basic side ("Successful Salesmanship," "Business Law"), but its potential for future development is vast. It not only can save an executive's time, it can simultaneously expand his mind. It is a toss-up which is more important to career growth.

Another, often ignored way to plug the time drain is by improving your listening power. "Communication" has become almost a fetish in business today. Executives, salesmen, foremen, everybody is urged to learn how to get across his message with maximum effectiveness. Ironically, almost no one seems to have realized that communication is a two-way street. The average businessman, who spends 70 percent of a typical day communicating, devotes 45 percent of that time to listening. Yet dismayingly few are *trained* to listen.

Researchers have demonstrated that the average individual, without training, forgets 42 percent of what he has just heard; at the end of an hour he has forgotten 56 percent; at the end of eight hours 64 percent. Long before a person reaches adult years, bad listening habits have been formed. The typical conversation (in both business and social life) involves one person waiting for the other to stop talking so that he can start. If he disagrees with the speaker, he hears (oddly) less of what is being said to him. But even when he agrees, once this fact registers, the average man's mind begins to wander.

The result is too often a monologue where there should be a dialogue—with inevitable frayed tempers, irate customers, and sulky workers.

Is there a cure? Xerox Corporation's newly formed education division thinks so, and so do I after hearing their "Effective Listening Course." Notice I said *hearing*. After studying how people listen, Xerox decided that the only way to root out bad listening habits, which are formed in childhood, was to make adults practice listening the right way. They have therefore concocted a course that is mostly on audio tape.

As much as possible, the tapes simulate real conversations. The fifty-nine statements in the program come at the trainee often mixed in with big-city background noises, and are spoken by a smorgasbord of vocal styles. Some voices are shrill and rapid, others slurred and low, some speak grammatically, others speak so ungrammatically they would turn a high school English teacher purple. Some ramble, others are clipped and precise. Beginning with simple statements such as "We can't use this cutter because the blade is too long," the lessons escalate to a final five-minute-long harangue. Trainees take quick tests in a response booklet, with the emphasis on *direct* answers.

Basically, if the Xerox researchers are right, effective listening is a matter of being able to capture and summarize essential information from what you hear. The best way to do this is by retaining mental "key word" outlines, sifting main from supporting points in a statement and learning to quickly recognize and dismiss irrelevant material. These comparatively simple rules, plus practice, have increased the listening power of one group of salesmen from a pretraining score of 20 percent to 84 percent, and sales managers from 51 to 91 percent.

Some twenty-five American companies have tried out the program, including IBM, RCA, Westinghouse, Sylvania, and General Dynamics. They have all found it extremely productive, especially with salesmen. Even more impressive is the enthusiasm of the trainees, who now number over 150,000. Perhaps most important, it creates genuine, new interest in communicating effectively—in both directions.

The question of time has other interesting ramifications. I dangled a $40,000-a-year job in front of an executive the other day. Naturally he was interested, but his first question was "Where?"

"New York," I said.

"I'll take it," he said, "if you can guarantee me what I've got here. Each night I'm home from work in fifteen minutes and five minutes later I'm out on the lake fishing."

"Sorry," I said, "I'm not a real estate developer."

Around the country there is growing an almost pathological dislike for executive jobs in big cities. Nobody wants to work in Los Angeles, Philadelphia, Chicago, or especially New York.

I'm afraid I can't blame them. New York, with its city income tax, its sky-high real estate, its antiquated transportation system, and its monumental traffic jams, is a kind of urban nightmare. And the other cities aren't far behind.

But for all its torments, I think a man who turns down a chance to tackle a big city is missing the challenge of a lifetime. Not just to his nervous system, but to his growth as an executive. Speaking as a North Carolinian who started his business career in Philadelphia, I can only say that there is an indefinable but nontheless real something about a metropolis that still makes it the major league as far as business is concerned. But so what? If there is one idea I am not afraid of repeating in this book, it is the need for every man to avoid ruts, to keep climbing, even if it's only out of a rut or over a molehill.

Something else about the big city that the modern businessman should consider: today, as never before, executives need experiences that broaden them. They need to be stimulated by new ideas, new people. They need to be able to express themselves with sophistication and polish. You can get a lot of these things in a major city. Monday you can lunch Chinese; Tuesday, French; Wednesday, Italian; Thursday, Spanish; and Friday, Greek. And all the nuances in between. French restaurants that specialize in the marvelous seafoods of Brittany or the haute cuisine of Paris or the specialties of the provinces. North Italian, Roman, and Neapolitan cooking become part of your vocabulary. You learn to handle a wine list without getting flustered.

All around you there is a continuous cultural fair: art exhibits, good museums, plays, concerts, and top universities where a younger man (or even an older man) can find the very latest business thinking expounded in the evening hours.

Fishing on a lake, golfing on uncrowded courses, hunting in the woods a half hour from home, I know how great these things are. Nobody loves the outdoors more than I. But I prefer to drive (or fly) a few extra hours to do my relaxing on weekends. I stay in the city and put up with the traffic, the smog. I tell other people to do the same thing if they get the chance. Believe it or not, it's worth it.

This brings us around to an equally thorny subject—vacations.

Not long ago a travel industry research organization reported in shocked tones that one out of every six American employees does *not* take the vacation for which he is eligible each year. Highest on this list of nontakers were executives and supervisors. Typical of these is a Chicago management consultant who hasn't taken a vacation more than three days long in nine years. "I love my work," he says. "I can't think of anything I would rather do."

Some psychologists maintain that such men are "workholics"—addicted to work like junkies are hooked on horse or boozers on the bottle. I say these headshrinkers are nuts.

Vacations have become an item of prime executive concern. Not to the men who take them so much as to the men who legislate them. Some companies now insist that every one of their executives take one week off for every six weeks they work. I think this is as silly as the headshrinkers with their notion of the compulsive worker.

At the same time, I am not against vacations. I think every man must learn how to get away from his job. Somewhere, sometime he must get a break, because routine in itself is a debilitating, mind-destroying thing. But *how* he gets that break is something that he should decide, not his company or the travel industry.

I take my own vacation each weekend during the winter, running a large resort and ski lodge I operate as a sideline in northern New York. Weekdays I spend at my desk, straining my brain to put the right man in the right job, running on the old, familiar treadmill of executive lunches and dinners, conferences and reports. When I go north I shed this executive skin, put on a woolen shirt and a fur hat, and charge up and down the slopes repairing lift lines, policing reckless skiers, shoveling snow over ice patches, and generally exhausting myself to the point where I sometimes fall asleep at the supper table. But it's a good, sound, physical sleep, and I often get twelve hours of it. (Not at the table.) When I get back to New York after one of these weekends, I am totally refreshed and raring to tackle the executive rat race again.

These are my vacations. Undoubtedly the Chicago management consultant has learned for himself that three days does the same trick for him. Perhaps playing golf or tennis or doing what another executive I know prefers—spending the weekend in bed—will do it for you.

Every time I have taken more than a one-week vacation, anywhere, I am crawling up the walls. It doesn't mean I'm a workholic, it means I enjoy my work so much I miss it.

There are some men who simply don't get along with their wives and children. To inflict a regular series of one-week vacations on them over the course of the year can demoralize and frustrate them so much they are in worse shape when they get back to their jobs. I know everyone *should* get along with his wife and children, but the simple fact is, not everyone meets the ideal requirements of the psychologists or the travel agents. Executives must learn to live in a very real, not an ideal world.

Executives aren't the only ones who don't see much point in extended vacations. A few years ago the steel union won thirteen-week sabbaticals every five years for its members. Salaried employees of the steel companies were offered a choice between the sabbaticals and a savings plan. Eighty percent of the salaried people at one corporation chose savings. This pattern of choice, rather than compulsion, should be the vacation style for executives in every company across the nation. Let each man work out his own vacation pattern with maximum flexibility and we will have happier, more productive managers off and on the job.

QUESTIONS
YOU MUST ANSWER

AT least a dozen times a month bewildered men appear in my office searching not for advancement but for survival, not for the challenge of a new job but for the mere security of a paycheck. These are defeated men.

Why are they defeated? Because they lost control of their careers. And why did they lose control? Because nine times out of ten they never stopped to take a career check-up. Let's take one now.

1. Have your goals changed? This is the biggest question you have to answer. One man I know never suspected he had an iota of executive talent. He saw himself as a specialist, a scientist. More or less by accident he got involved in politics in his suburb. Before he knew what was happening, he found himself organizing a political campaign. He got such a kick out of it, his enthusiasm and self-confidence carried over into the business world. He jumped out of the

laboratory into an office and today is a major executive with a drug company.

Other men scale down goals which may have been too grandiose. One friend recently amazed me by confessing that until recently he considered himself only "halfway there." He owned his own company, which had a comfortable niche in his particular industry. But all these years his real ambition was to be the biggest, the best, to dominate the industry. Now he had changed his mind. "Life is too short," he said. "If I stayed in my office until midnight seven nights a week for the next twenty years I think I could do it. But I've decided I want to leave my children more than an inheritance tax problem."

2. Has your company changed *its* goals since you entered it? Has it shifted from the single-industry concept to diversification on a grand scale? Has it exchanged stability for expansion? How do these changes fit your personality? Your goals? Are you pursuing stability, corporate peace of mind, while those around you are vigorously pursuing change? Has the company, on the other hand, gone through a period of rapid expansion and now entered the digestion process where stability, not growth, is the goal? Have you been bucking this tide, charging out in search of new frontiers?

3. Has the company changed in other ways? Is there a youth movement afoot—at a point in your career when you are just a little too old to qualify? Has the company become hypnotized by foreign business to the point where all promotions go to men who have overseas experience? Has it shifted from the committee to individual form of leadership

136

or vice versa? Again you have to ask yourself, "How do I fit into this new pattern?"

4. What are your resources? There are two kinds of career resources: (a) that blend of experience and talent which we call executive know-how; (b) your net worth. Every executive should ask himself regularly whether he is acquiring the breadth and depth necessary to go to the top in today's business world. Failure to acquire these skills and the tendency to stay too long in a job that is rewarding financially but narrow in terms of experience are the two main reasons for the career crisis that strikes so many American executives in their mid-forties and early fifties. As for net worth, too many businessmen think of it only when they reach the outskirts of retirement years. A tragic mistake, when we consider the tremendous opportunities executives have to acquire substantial capital today. But this won't be done by the man who spends his entire career in one company, plugging along on his salary. He may, through a corporate savings plan, build up a wonderful nest egg for his golden years, but he will not acquire money early enough to give him what I call creative mobility.

These are the broad outlines of a career checkup. The specifics must, of course, be filled in by you. I guarantee you it is worth the time and trouble.

You don't have to wait until your career is in full bloom to take a checkup. You can do it before you even start work, thanks to Ross R. Millhiser, president of Philip Morris Domestic. In a speech he recently gave to students at Georgetown University, Millhiser outlined one of the best rating sheets I have heard of in years.

The key word in Millhiser's vocabulary is effectiveness. No matter how complex business becomes, the man who can get results will still run the show. "Without his ability," Millhiser points out, "other desirable and even rare characteristics remain unproductive." What makes for effectiveness? Here is what he looks for:

1. Ability to solve problems.
2. Capacity for work.
3. Ability to communicate thoughts, written as well as oral.
4. Intelligence.
5. Perseverance, tenacity, and resiliency.

How can a young man rate his problem-solving ability? One way, in Millhiser's opinion, is "breaking the grade barrier in all the subjects he takes." This, he insists, is *the* major problem a young man has to solve in college or high school. The pattern used to break this grade barrier is, he believes, not significantly different from the one the executive uses to solve business problems. Basically both the student and the executive must learn to synthesize. The student synthesizes his own observations and what Millhiser calls "the input of his professors, the output of his source material." In business the executive synthesizes "the activity and contributions of his associates and those who report to him."

Millhiser sees no need to worry about the argument about the liberal arts background and the strictly vocational course. If you break the grade barrier in either one you are synthesizing and that is what counts.

Discussing capacity for work, Millhiser makes another telling point. This phrase does not mean the ability to produce furious outbursts of energy. On the contrary, it means "you must be able to deliver over an extended period of time."

The ability to communicate is an essential part of the executive's synthesizing role. To put his ideas into effect, he must be able to explain them simply and clearly. "This is the difference between the superintellectual specialist," Mr. Millhiser says, "and the effective executive, who is essentially a leader, not a technician."

As for intelligence, Millhiser says one does not need to be a double dome to synthesize. And as many an executive has learned to his dismay when he hired someone simply on the basis of a graduate school of business degree, "extraordinary intelligence does not guarantee good judgment and common sense."

Millhiser's last category, perseverance, tenacity, and resilience, underscores points he has already made. "So many people of extraordinary ability," he says, "simply do not have staying power. If they strike out early in the game, they fold. If they don't go ahead as fast as they think they should, or don't receive their just due on their own timetable, they fold. All of this is related to that capacity for work."

Summing up, he adds (and I could not agree with him more), "Unalloyed intelligence receives too much weighting in selecting who should occupy what jobs and who should go to which college today."

That perennial problem of money is another question you have to answer, especially when it is put in the following blunt terms: Are you underpaid?

A small electronics company in the Midwest has never quite recovered from the day the paychecks got mixed up. Due to a clerical error, 120 employees received paychecks meant for fellow workers. Engineers who were doing much the same work suddenly discovered that one of their number was making $3,000 a year more than they were. Secretaries who sat side by side and typed similar reports were paid anywhere from sixty-five to ninety-five dollars a week. In some instances, persons who had served the company loyally for a decade were drawing smaller paychecks than employees of a year or less. A star salesman who had been assured he was getting the top salary in the department found out he was near the bottom on the pay scale. He quit on the spot. Within three months, there was a one-fifth turnover in personnel. Small wonder that the best-kept secret in the business community is who makes how much.

Just what percentage of our labor force is underpaid?

I checked three employment specialists: one said that 15 percent of the persons who came to him were underpaid; another put the figure at 10 percent; a third asserted that the figure varied from industry to industry, from company to company, adding that "as many as half the personnel in some companies are underpaid." Personally, I would cast my vote with the third man.

Is there a plot on the part of management to underpay certain people? By and large, no. Most companies strive to reward employees according to their work. They realize how seriously salary inequities undermine employee relations. Many companies will even pay a beginner "more than the going price" to gain a reputation for generosity.

However, inequities do develop. The personnel director of a large printing plant once told me, "One out of every ten employees here is underpaid and about one out of ten is overpaid. Part of my job is to remedy this situation."

A basic reason for underpayment is the "we knew you when" syndrome. A man starts working for a company at $75 a week. Ten years later he is making $10,000 a year. In terms of his progress within the company he has done well. But frequently people on his level in other companies are making $12,000 to $14,000 a year.

Today, however, more and more people are beginning to realize that numbers do not tell the whole salary story. Fringe benefits and something I call "psychic income" should also be added into a paycheck. I know one man, a father of six, who has turned down several better-paying jobs because his company offers scholarships to employees' children. "When I hear my friends worry about college tuition I can just sit back and smile," he says.

The personnel director of a big advertising agency says, "Compared with some of our competitors, 90 percent of our people are underpaid. But when you compare working conditions, you find that our people are treated a lot better. One man came here from a rough but high-paying competitor who had almost ruined his health. He was working at about 50 percent of capacity when our office manager suggested that he take a month's rest at company expense. He returned a different man and one of the agency's biggest boosters. We care about people around here."

A salesman in a Philadelphia department store was thinking of quitting to take a $500 raise with a sales manufacturing agent. Then he sat down and with a little arithmetic discovered that his employee discount added $500 to his salary each year, and he was completely disregarding it.

This cautionary attitude is important. It is painful to see people go through the turmoil of a job change and get little or nothing in return. But in the long run, risking or at least exploring job change is the only sure way a man can find out if he is getting his real value on the job market. It takes courage to discover your salary potential, but when you look at it from the viewpoint of a working lifetime, it can mean as much as $100,000 in total earnings, and that sum well invested can be the difference between a comfortable and a strapped retirement. Most of the time discovering the truth is a positive, creative, liberating experience. I always remember the words of a man who, after twenty years with the same company, had just switched to a competitor and added $5,000 to his income. "When I found out what I was really worth, I realized for the first time what these words in the Bible meant—the truth shall make you free."

IDEAS THAT MOVE MEN

L ET me tell you a tale of two young executives.

The first is Clif Eaton, a vice-president of the Gillette Company. Clif acquired his know-how via "learning by doing." His company gave him startling amounts of responsibility almost from the day he walked in the door. He made mistakes, of course; he was supposed to learn from them.

I often think of Clif in combination with another old friend, who learned the executive trade in precisely the opposite fashion. His company believes in learning by watching, listening, asking questions—but not by doing. That came later. At one time this second friend—let's call him Fred—looked at least as promising as Clif Eaton.

Yet Fred never made it to the top. I lost track of him years ago, but I am sure he is wandering in the middle-level doldrums somewhere. What does it mean? Can we conclude from this that learning by doing is better than learning by watching? If I said that I would be swimming against a veritable tidal wave of big-company opinion.

No, I am more inclined to conclude that it is not systems, but men that make the business world move. And for me, the crucial factor in two equally matched pacers on the executive track is desire. By that I *don't* mean *What Makes Sammy Run*-type grabbiness, but the steady, unremitting wish to *achieve*. This is the fuel injector that makes the difference between the executive and the run-of-the-mill model.

I spent years puzzling over why one man has it and another doesn't. Recently I came across the best answer I have yet seen, in the work of Professor David C. McClelland at Harvard. McClelland has spent seventeen years probing the mystery of achievement. His findings suggest that achievers are not simply born that way, but acquire their traits from special training they get in the home, from parents who set "moderately high achievement goals but who are warm, encouraging, and nonauthoritarian in helping these children reach these goals." This early experience creates in these individuals a *need* for achievement. They spend their time thinking about doing things better.

McClelland has taken samples of such men's spontaneous thoughts and from them has created a test which enables him to score or rate the amount of a man's "N-ach," as he calls it.

"When other people begin to think in N-ach terms, things begin to move," McClelland says. "Men with higher N-ach get more raises and are promoted more rapidly because they keep actively seeking ways to do a better job. Companies with many such men grow faster."

McClelland has extended his research in this area from individuals to whole countries. "A nation which is thinking about doing better all the time actually does do better economically speaking," he says. He has made studies which show this to be true in ancient Greece, in Spain in the Middle Ages, and in England from 1400 to 1800, as well as among contemporary nations, capitalist or communist, developed or underdeveloped.

Since 1960 McClelland and his research team have been experimenting with techniques to increase achievement-oriented thinking. They've brought in individuals with low ratings and taught them to think, talk, and act like persons with high N-ach. The course has stimulated these men to set higher but carefully planned and realistic work goals for themselves over the next two years. And a high proportion of them achieved these goals.

It would seem, then, for the first time, we don't have to lapse into mysticism to explain why the Clif Eatons of this world succeed. Thanks to McClelland's creative research, we can actually pinpoint what makes executives go, and we can produce this go power in men who don't have it. This could be one of the major breakthroughs in American business history.

Personnel men are, in my opinion, the chief roadblock to unleashing this N-ach potential.

Recently the president of a company in very serious trouble asked me to conduct an urgent search for a sales vice-president with an unusual blend of scientific depth and executive drive. Our month-long search produced three first-rate possibilities, and I called the president to ask him when he wanted to see them.

"I'm awfully busy right now," he said. "I'd like my personnel man to screen them first."

I like to think I was speaking for all the members of the executive search field when I told him in reply, "Do you seriously think these men, all line executives making over $30,000 a year, are going to let a $10,000-a-year staff man pass judgment on them?"

The president quickly changed his mind and agreed to interview them personally. But his initial reaction was lamentably typical. In too many American companies top men shun what I consider the most important part of their job. They don't hire people. They leave that vital, but often troublesome function to the personnel department. In my opinion, this is not only dereliction of executive duty, it is creeping suicide.

Personnel men undoubtedly perform a useful function in hiring clerical help and other routine employees. They screen out those with bad work histories, criminal records, obvious psychological maladjustments. For routine jobs it is probably a good thing to hire more or less average people. But for executives, this average, well-adjusted Sunday school image of the nice person is hopelessly wrong.

The executive is by definition an individualist. He wants, in fact needs, the chance to demonstrate this individuality, this creativity, when he tackles the job. Part of being an executive is an ability to recognize this creativity in a man sitting opposite you. In a half-hour interview the good executive should be able to sense with an intuition that goes beyond logic (and psychological tests) whether a man will fit his company's style, whether he is, in a word, *simpatico*.

I believe that a working executive should be prepared to spend 25 percent of his time searching out new talent. He can only do this by keeping a scorecard, constantly moving around his industry, going to conventions and institutes, meeting the other executives in his field, and working, when necessary, with executive search firms. Finally, he must regularly indulge in that moment of truth, the hiring interview. He must take the responsibility for hiring a man— which means the responsibility for what that man does in the company, or to the company. It isn't easy; it may involve making big mistakes which can only be rectified by firing the mistake maker. But firing is simply the other side of hiring. It is like birth and death. You cannot have one without the other.

Sounds tough, I know. But we might consider for a moment the cruelties in the other approach. I have sent thousands of executives to corporate interviews and can tell you from experience how many men came away seething with humiliation when they found themselves being judged by a personnel man who made one fourth their salary. An executive deserves something better than this assembly line treatment. It is like asking a pussycat for an opinion of a lion. The pussycat is bound to judge the king of beasts on its own terms. Executives are a breed apart. They deserve to be judged only by cats of their own size, speed, and strength.

Now you know how important I think it is for executives—upper, middle, and lower middle—to do their own hiring and firing. It is the other side of the coin I was selling in the opening pages, when I urged job seekers to avoid personnel men wherever possible.

Does it work? For an answer, let me tell you the saga of Chesterton Packing and Seals, the nation's oldest manufacturer of mechanical packing (sophisticated rope to contain fluids, gases, or slurries carried by pumps and other hydraulic equipment). Today Chesterton ranks among the leaders in a $200-million-a-year industry, and in terms of growth it ranks No. 1.

How do they do it? By looking for what I call the "buck smeller," the money-hungry, profit-minded man who doesn't care whether people like him or not and shies away from supervision. Chesterton executives find these men themselves. Experience has convinced them that no personnel man with his batteries of psychological tests can do the job. Believe it or not, Chesterton's executives even go onto campuses to seek out prospects. It goes without saying that these busy men do not have time to give written tests or ponder answers to involved questionnaires.

Chesterton executives are primarily interested in a man's motivation. Does he want early executive responsibility, quick advancement, and earnings well above average? Then he is their man. Ironically, in our conformist and security-conscious world Chesterton is having trouble finding men with these traits. James D. Chesterton, manager of international sales, said recently, "The college placement directors we work with screen carefully all their candidates to meet our company's requirements, but recent graduates don't appear to be the material we need."

A classic Chesterton story concerns a Boston University graduate who asked his alumni office to help him get out of the drug business into something "safer." The placement officer told him about Chesterton but warned him that safety was no consideration in the company's thinking.

It should be no surprise that the man's first Chesterton interview was a disaster. So was his second. But a week later the young man called to ask for a third interview. This time Chesterton assigned a different executive, and he too labeled the fellow a security hunter—and that was an automatic blackball at Chesterton. To their amazement, however, the man called for another interview. When it was refused he camped in the company reception area for a day and a half.

Finally the general sales manger, Richard T. McDermott, decided "to see why he was so persistent and if this persistence could be transferred to our advantage." In his office Mr. McDermott discovered a different man from the security hunter who had turned up for the first interview. His contact with Chesterton executives had literally changed his entire outlook. Now, he told McDermott, he realized that "nothing is free, you have to work for it. I've looked around and I think I can do it. Most of all, I want to show you and the other people around here that if you don't take me on you'll be missing out on something great."

McDermott hired him on the spot. The young man has

since been delivering magnificently in a fiercely competitive territory. Why? Because he had a chance to meet some real executives and this contact with reality was like an injection of supervitamins. Would he have gotten the same thing from a series of psychological tests?

Recently I have seen signs of significant changes in personnel thinking.

I spent half of one recent day talking with the directors of personnel for two of the nation's biggest corporations. I came away with the conviction that a new era in American business may well be sliding through the door. Real changes usually make their appearance quietly.

Since World War II personnel men have been the employees' advocate on the management team. They sold management on the idea that by giving employees everything from baseball teams to ski resorts they could create a happier company. They preached the idea of the company as a family, and to make sure that the children were compatible, they used psychological tests aimed at finding Mr. Average and weeding out the maverick and individualists.

This image of business as a kind of love affair has failed to work, and it startled me to hear personnel men admitting it. "I'm not interested in what the employee wants from the company," one of these personnel directors told me. "I'm only interested in what the company can *get* from him. Basically I don't even like the term 'personnel director.' I see myself as a human assets comptroller. It's my job to supervise $57 million worth of human assets and make sure the company gets a good return on its investment in each man."

"I'm not around to pump the milk of human kindness

into people," said the other man. "I'm working for the *company*, and I make it very clear to everyone I hire that I expect the same attitude from them."

Nodding in emphatic agreement, the first man added, "I don't care much about a man's psychological profile as long as he does his job well. We have hired people with personal problems which would bar them at other average-minded companies. I contend personal problems are none of the company's business—unless they interfere with work. If they do—it's goodbye Charlie."

Summing up, the second man said, "Manpower planning is simply part of the overall business planning a company does each year."

This is tough talk, but I happen to know the talkers mean it. Both of them have been mavericks with not very impressive scholastic records (but good war records), always very receptive to unorthodox ideas. Maybe they are exceptional—so exceptional they stand alone. But I don't think so.

I have seen how this new approach has delighted the executives in their companies, and I have seen how it is paying off for the companies in better performance up and down the line. With the current squeeze on profits from unions and taxes, more and more executives are switching from the "give them something" philosophy of the earlier generation of personnel men, and now some of the best personnel men are frankly admitting it was a mistake and probably a waste of money from the start.

The "give them" philosophy weakens a company where it needs to be strong—in the profit and loss column. I am all for giving employees what they earn from increased productivity. But giving people something for nothing does not impress them. It only makes them suspicious and more difficult to handle.

On the job at all levels of business, this new hard-nosed philosophy should be a bracing blast of fresh air for those who are ready to earn their way with achievement. The days of coasting along on a cushion of easy profits are over. More and more companies are getting down on the hard, cold, realistic ground, where everybody has to take off his coat and get a little dirty. And it looks as if the personnel men will be right there in the middle of the scramble, like that old West Point coach who used to scrimmage with his players, yelling, "Blood. I want to see some blood!"

I became aware of another significant sign of change in the personnel world during a visit I had recently from an old friend, director of personnel for a major Midwest corporation. He came to me in search of advice, because he was frightened, harried, and in danger of losing his job. The company's management training program was exploding in his face, and the president was sputtering like a bomb upstairs. What was wrong, he asked, morosely flipping a portfolio describing the program, which he had spread on my desk. They paid one of the highest starting salaries in the nation. The program did not last too long, in contrast to some of their competitors' programs. Company X, for instance, had people still grinding away on the training level three years after they entered the firm. Why, they even avoided the word "trainee." Instead, they called their boys "consultants." Yet they were quitting in droves, and the ones that stayed did not seem to have the drive of an anemic gnat.

"That's your trouble," I said, "that word 'consultants.' "

"Why?"

"You're giving them dreams of glory before they even know how to sharpen a pencil."

I was speaking from experience. I know another company that had made the identical mistake, even down to the word. I think it is symptomatic of a lot of things that trouble me in business today. Too many corporations are so worried about pleasing the bright young types coming out of college today that they are bending and even breaking fundamental psychological rules. You don't win a man's respect, much less his affection, by handing him titles, or even money, on a platter. As we are learning to our distress in the poverty program, such tactics only encourage disrespect and even contempt.

Again, these tactics amaze me because they run contrary to the experience of the men who are in charge of today's corporations. Get any group of old-timers together and you will inevitably hear them reminisce about a previous president or general manager who was a tough, mean, opinionated slave driver. Working for him, they hated his guts, but now in the golden glow of memory they remember what he gave them—a sense of genuine achievement. "I learned more from that old son of a gun in a year than I'd learned in the previous ten," they will say.

They don't seem to realize it, but they are looking back on a psychological experience which the Marine Corps and, to a lesser extent, the Army have used for decades. Marine boot camp is still as harrowing as a mother-conscious Congress will permit. A man who comes through it has a sense of personal pride and self-confidence which he may have lacked before. He also, it should be noted, has a fierce loyalty to the Corps.

I am not suggesting that business today should try to reproduce the Marine boot camp experience in their training programs, any more than they should follow literally the examples of the slave drivers of yesteryear. We have to be realistic. But I am convinced that every company should insist that its trainees will be known by no other name and that they should get some grease under their fingernails whenever and wherever possible. Promising a man too much, even by implication, is a kind of betrayal.

Not only should the company avoid the syndrome, but the young man starting out should be extra wary of it. In the end, when he takes a nothing job with a phony title he only cheats himself. The kind of confidence that makes for success in business today is rooted in self-respect, and this invaluable ingredient can only be acquired through genuine achivement. No matter how much a man may try to kid himself, he knows, when he looks in the mirror, whether he accomplished anything worthwhile in the previous week, month, or year.

If the answer is nothing, he should get out of the company like Tarzan with his loincloth on fire. When it comes to wasted careers, there is no point in passing the buck to a mistaken corporate policy.

The trouble is, each generation of businessmen forgets

too easily what the previous generation learned, often at painful expense. Running for a plane recently, I grabbed a book off a shelf. It turned out to be a collection of speeches by Charles F. Kettering that someone had given me years ago and I had never read. At first I was annoyed, but when I started turning the pages I changed my mind. Reading these remarks by the genius who was for a generation head of research at General Motors, I realized that no matter how much business changes, there are certain core truths that don't change—and we need to hang on to these while we ride the economic roller coaster.

A few pages back I wrote about the importance of desire. Twenty years ago Kettering summed it up in a sentence. "I want the man who wants to do something. He is the one I am interested in."

Among my major growls is the tendency for management consultants and personnel men to rely on the so-called expert. Kettering told the Chamber of Commerce of the United States in 1929, "There is a type of individual in the world that I don't have much use for, and that is the expert. If I want to stop a research program, I can always do it by getting a few experts to sit in on the subject, because they know right away that it was a fool thing to try in the first place."

By now you know that I believe in encouraging mavericks, individualists, brash young men with new ideas. But I get a lot of discouraged letters from these types, telling me how often their new ideas get slapped down. Thirty years ago Kettering had an answer to that too. "When you present a new idea its history is as definite as the history of a silkworm. You lay the new idea on the table, and they push it off into the wastebasket. Do not get discouraged at that. That is only the first time they pushed it off. Just get to that wastebasket before the janitor."

Among my favorite alarm bells is the one that I keep ringing about corporations and executives that get fat and complacent. Here's Kettering: "I have said before that self-satisfaction is one of the world's worst diseases. That is especially so in business."

Other Kettering gems:

"Some people like to plan too exactly and you can't plan exactly. You have to plan with a broad scope. You have seen these systematic types of persons who say, 'We've got that fixed. Let's fasten it down.' I call such people 'hot riveters.' As soon as they get a situation set up, they want to rivet it— make it permanent, so to speak."

"I think that every once in a while we ought to analyze ourselves to find out how much more we may be worth to the company by staying away than by coming to work."

"The greatest mistake of all is to do nothing."

SO WHAT IF
YOU'RE FIRED

I WAS fired from my last job. At the time I thought it
was the worst catastrophe of the twentieth century. It was a
familiar story. I had bustled into this small company and
spouted all sorts of new ideas at the boss. I saw ways to
expand, diversify, grow. The boss didn't want to grow. He
was perfectly happy taking no risks and making a modest
profit. Finally, he decided I was sowing dissension and dissatisfaction among the other salesmen and he fired me.

I was frantic. How do you get another job if you've
been fired? I felt as if the mark of Cain had been branded
on my forehead. Finally, after a week of brooding I tried for
a comeback. With sweating palms I sat down in the office of
a prospective employer and heard him ask the question I
dreaded. "Why did you leave your last job?"

I took a deep breath and plunged in. "I got fired," I
said, and then I explained in detail why the boss and I had

clashed. I was hired, and I haven't been fired since, thank God. But I still think the principle I followed, more or less by instinct and on the spur of the moment, is sound. I had cooked up a half-dozen elaborate lies which wouldn't have fooled my new boss for five minutes. Now, knowing how easy it is to check a man's story of why he left a previous job, I am more than ever convinced that honesty is the only policy.

Even if a man has been fired for theft, embezzlement, or drinking, I think the best thing to do is tell the truth, and accompany it, of course, with a firm statement that now things are different with you. But the vast majority of firings are not caused by those kinds of human foibles, they are usually the result of a personality clash with the boss which has embarrassed him within the department or in the company at large. This is the one infallible way to get fired today in American business (rather than transferred or demoted). Such clashes are often no reflection on a man's talent, though if they happen too often they may cast some doubt upon his judgment. There is no reason why they can't be discussed fully and frankly with another employer.

One smart young man I know actually made getting fired a very positive and highly effective sales pitch for his next job. He went around telling people what he'd learned from getting fired, and he soon had offers from a half-dozen better openings.

He proved conclusively that the fact of getting fired is almost irrelevant. Why you got fired is the crucial matter. Sometimes it is a testimony to a man's superiority rather than his inferiority. Often it gives the man a much needed kick in the pants. One top executive told me recently, "When I was twenty-five I was one of the world's lousiest salesmen. I should have been fired. I wasted three years, just coasting along, because I had a complacent boss and a complacent, profitable company. Only when we hit a recession and the going got really tough, did I realize how much I hadn't learned."

If and when the ax does fall you may be consoled by another fact. These days presidents of companies get fired more often than anybody else, except baseball managers.

As president of the National Association of Executive Recruiters, I attract résumés the way the proverbial honey jar draws flies. On a single day fifty—even a hundred—is not an unusual number. With these career histories come letters which resound with a single cry. *How do I get a job, fast?*

It is a terribly human question. No one wants to endure the anxiety of joblessness one second longer than necessary. Unfortunately this uneasiness drives too many people to look for instant remedies, usually dispensed by well-meaning friends. "Fire out 5,000 résumés," one man says. "One of them is bound to hit." "Go to one employment agency and throw yourself on their mercy," another suggests. "Talk to management consultants," guarantees a third. "Executive recruiters have the inside track," assures a fourth pundit.

The harried victim, clutching for the feeling if not the substance of security, bets his all on one of these remedies. Result: he is out of work far longer than if he tackled the job search in a precisely opposite frame of mind, accepting the hard, but not necessarily frightening conclusion: *there are no shortcuts.*

There is just no substitute for a systematic approach to the job search. After watching thousands do it, I think I can with some authority suggest the following order of priority.

1. The classified ads. The newspaper remains the greatest of all shortcuts in job hunting. It is the one way in which an employer in search of a man can communicate with the maximum number of people. Every job searcher or would-be job changer should read the ads religiously.

2. Employment agencies. Well-established agencies are almost as important from this broad communication viewpoint. They focus opportunities, and the job searcher should canvass as many as possible.

3. Direct mail. This rates third place because the area of opportunity is necessarily narrower. I have by now, I hope, made more than clear my preference for the rifle shot over the machine-gun-5,000-mimeographed-résumés approach. But in terms of probable payoffs, this approach could easily be ranked No. 1.

4. Personal contact. Fourth, because it is narrower still. It can be potent if used carefully. But don't sit back and rely on a single man.

5. Executive recruiters. They are this far down the list because they do not search for jobs, they search for men. The companies hire them, and only by coincidence can the needs of job searcher and executive searcher coincide. The average recruiter, moreover, can rarely handle more than six or eight searches at one time. So if you want to know

how many available jobs a single firm has on tap, just multiply their total staff by six. Since most staffs are fairly small, the wise job seeker will *not* rely on a single firm.

6. Management consultants. Forget them.

Following these priorities and eventually, if necessary, bringing all of them into play, you can substantially reduce the out-of-work screaming meemies. It's like betting on all the horses in the race. Not a bad idea, when it's a race you can't afford to lose.

You may be surprised by how high I put employment agencies in this list of priorities. Until recently I have been a little condescending toward this job route. I've always included them in my public discussions of the job search, but it was usually toward the bottom of the list, with a "just in case" or "last resort" tone.

No more. As the number of managers expands, employment agencies are becoming more and more important for the man in search of an opening in the middle and lower middle management range. Moreover, the agencies themselves have become much more sophisticated in their approach to the job search. A new company recently formed by the merger of five New York agencies is typical of this new approach. They have specialists in fields such as electronic data processing, accounting, investments, insurance, and (significant again) retail management, engineering, and hotel management. In 1964 this company earned a mere $1000 in fees from engineering placements. In the year ending March 31, 1968, this jumped to $81,000. Accounting placements jumped from $36,000 to $252,000. No less than seventy of the jobs they placed in the electronic data processing field in 1968 were on the executive level, and there were another fifty in hotel management.

This company calls its interviewers "employment counselors" and it actually prefers to recruit people without previous employment agency experience. They have their own training program, which lasts from three months to a year, depending on the "technical difficulties" of the specialty. During this time the trainee works as an assistant to a senior counselor and is thoroughly grounded in interviewing, client relations, advertising, and (another significant word) recruiting.

This company and other agencies of similar caliber are edging into the executive recruiting field. Thus far the company has pretty much limited itself to the data processing business, where it has considerable expertise. Executive recruiting fees last year were a modest $54,000, but this will probably grow. So will their job horizons. Recruiting will give them opportunities to understand a company's needs on a deeper, more intimate level.

Gone is the day when the employment agency dealt almost exclusively in secretaries, clerks, and an occasional office manager. There is real gold, genuine opportunity, in those mountains of ads they run each week. The smart job seekers these days will visit them *first*—instead of last. Not only is there a good chance of finding the answer to his economic prayers, he may also do it free of charge. More and more often, companies pay the fee for jobs where experience and skill are at a premium.

The job search is like a military campaign. The strategy

has to be sound. We have just discussed that in the outline of where to look. But the tactics are equally important. If you maneuver your enemy into a corner and then don't know how to use armor, artillery, and infantry, you will get walloped. In the job search, tactics come into play in that crucial encounter, the interview.

I will always remember a man named Foster who walked into my office in search of a job. He was well dressed and in the morning he probably looked crisp and efficient. But now it was 4:30 on a hot day in May, and his collar had wilted, his tie was crumpled, and his suit was sagging in the wrong places. As if I had pressed a button (which I hadn't), he began reciting. "Until February of this year I was employed as vice-president of marketing at . . ." I sighed and wondered for the 150th time why more executives didn't have the foggiest notion of how to conduct a successful job interview.

This man was like all the others. After he recited his résumé, he stopped and sat there, as defenseless as a Vietnamese civilian before a well-armed Vietcong, waiting for me to begin my third degree. No wonder (aside from the heat) his palms were moist with sweat and his eyelid twitched as we shook hands. Because he followed this routine, every interview was a horrible third degree from which he emerged feeling skinned alive.

What explains it? I've puzzled over it for hours, and I think the explanation goes back to the early days of the average executive's career. Then he came in, humble and practically crawling, ready to take any crumb that was swept off the rug for him. The moment he finds himself in the job-seeking seat, he reverts instantly to this cringing role.

What should he be doing? That old military maxim, the best defense is a good offense, is equally true in the interview situation. Instead of reciting his résumé, he should casually slip it into the interviewer's desk. Then he should start asking questions about the company that he is proposing to join. What is the profit picture? Is it family-owned, and if so what effect does this have on promotion policy? Why aren't more men promoted from within? Why does the plant in Dubuque look so dilapidated? How about stock options and other important forms of executive compensation? These are just a small sample of the almost infinite variety of questions a man can ask.

I'm not suggesting he should dominate the interview so completely that the man in the hiring seat never gets a chance to ask a question. But he should do enough talking to convey a positive, forceful presence. It is suicide to sit there and wait for the other fellow to throw the darts.

Simultaneously he should remember that he is walking and sitting in a house of mirrors. No movement or gesture will go unnoticed. The color of his socks and tie and shirt, the cut of his clothes, everything will be weighed in the balance. Only if he is the dominant personality in the encounter can he hope to hold his own.

At the same time, there is no harm in admitting a certain nervousness. If a man's palms are a little sweaty, so what? The interviewer expects it. But if he pauses before he shakes hands to wipe his hand on his pants, he has called attention to his anxiety, even made it a focal point of the interview. He has one strike against him before the fellow even throws the first fast ball at him.

The wise job seeker will schedule all his interviews early in the morning when he is fresh, and so are his clothes. He will avoid late-afternoon interviews and, if possible, interviews over lunch.

What is wrong with lunch? There is a tendency to get too relaxed. Inevitably liquor will be served, and this can make a man drop his guard even more. Gradually a man may lose that sense of drama, encounter, that enables him to project himself with the intensity and drive that spells success. Eventually, of course, there will be lunches and more extensive conferences, but the first interview is that moment of truth when a man communicates the essential that intrigues an employer into saying to himself, "I want this guy." It is too important to do it any way but the right way.

Another fallacy of the fired was proclaimed to my irritated ears a few months ago when a man confronted me across the desk in my office and proclaimed, "I want this to be my last job."

He had just turned fifty. Practically on his birthday he had been eased out of a good job as the result of a merger, and he was still a little shocked by the experience. He had never been fired before.

"I predict that you will have at least three jobs before you retire," I told him bluntly. "And moreover, I think you *should* have at least this many."

He blanched, sure he was talking to a nut.

But there is nothing nutty about what I told him, considering today's job atmosphere. Both companies and executives have jumped on the job-switching merry-go-round, and it is up to every man to ride it just as far as it will take him—always with a weather eye to the big brass ring, the stock option deal that can eliminate worries about the next job.

What explains it? The explosive growth of our economy in the last fifteen years, if you want it in one sentence. New technologies, new markets, appear overnight, creating "instant obsolesence" for whole groups of executives. They move out and others move in—or up. Also important is the steady growth of executive confidence. More and more men have proved they can switch industries and put their executive talents to work with the same effectiveness.

On the other side, companies which in the past would carry along a slipping executive today have no hesitation whatsoever about replacing him. A recent study showed that well over half the 250 largest American corporations used executive recruiters to bring in new talent during the past five years.

Hardly a day passes without a well-paid, apparently secure executive appearing at my door to slip his résumé into my files. He isn't looking around, oh no—but just in case I have something that sounds interesting . . .

I sometimes worry a little about what this trend is doing to older concepts such as company loyalty and executive responsibility. But realism is the first law of success, and so I must dutifully report to you, my readers, that he who bounces around these days has a far better chance of eventually bounding up the ladder.

In the past the man who had four or five job changes in ten years was often classified as unstable. Today the in-the-know company president welcomes such evidence on a résumé. It could be a sign that he's got a savvy, aggressive swinger here.

It took another hour of conversation, but I finally convinced my fifty-year-old friend to abandon his all-or-nothing attitude toward his next job and accept the facts of executive life. Within a month I had moved him into a job with a home products division of a fast-growing electronics company. But I told him—and this time he listened—"In three years don't be surprised if you've given this outfit all they can take from you. Right now they want someone who can stabilize them after a lot of wild growth. But in three years they'll be ready to take off on another spurt—and they may start looking around for a guy who can ride a runaway.

"If that happens, don't get excited. Just come back and see me. There'll be plenty of other people looking for a steady hand on the wheel."

Away he went, no longer scared. That's one thing I like about this new executive style. It takes guts to handle it.

THE MOST ASKED
QUESTIONS

MY syndicated column "On the Job" brings me a vast amount of queries about business dilemmas. Here are the questions that come up again and again with minor variations, and my answers.

I'm twenty-one, just out of college, and have an offer from a big corporation and another offer from a small, family-held company. Which should I take?

I can't decide for you. It depends on how you evaluate yourself. Does your personality need big-company prestige? Do you fit into a big-organization environment without undue stress and strain? Study yourself a little. If you went through high school and college without joining very many groups, if you haven't enjoyed extracurricular activities, if you don't particularly like the idea of being on a "team," your chances of performing well in a big corporation are slim. If there is something of the lone wolf in you, if you

169

like to do a lot of jobs simultaneously, accept plenty of solo responsibility—you will get a chance to practice this in a small company. One thing I do urge: *decide now.* Don't waste a year finding out what should be obvious with a little self-analysis.

Will joining the Peace Corps after I graduate from college hurt my business career?

Nothing will mortally wound your business career for your first two years out of college. The Peace Corps experience might even help it. It should broaden and sophisticate you and equip you to meet challenges, build up your self-confidence. But if you get so entranced with government service that you stay on for an additional two or three years, you will be hurting your career. From about the age of twenty-seven on a man's success is measured by his earnings. And you don't build a salary up to an impressive level overnight.

I've done pretty well in college, and had some interesting job offers. But I keep wondering, should I go on to a graduate school of business? My father can afford it.

Ten years ago I would have said no. Today I'm inclined to say the opposite, especially if you are the type of person who enjoys working for a large name corporation. The graduate school of business is the best place to learn how to move inside these big organizations, which have completely adopted the sophisticated mathematics-oriented, computer-based approach to organization and decision making. The graduate school of business will teach you how to speak their language—a language which is getting more specialized and recondite every day. Without this language you will have a difficult time making it to the top level of our corporate giants.

I'm a perfect sphere, rolling in no direction with a college diploma in my hand. How can I decide on a career?

Go back and find out what other people think about you. Your yearbook might be a good place to start. The off-hand comments classmates scribble in there are often excellent evaluations of how you impressed other people. Go back and talk to one or two of your teachers in college, or even in high school. Talk to your best friend. Above all, ask yourself bluntly if your main interest is making a large amount of money. A great many people have been led astray by guidance counselors and other advice givers until they are befuddled about just what goal they should pursue. Unless you have an overwhelming interest in the intellectual life, a passion to teach, write, paint, act—a very large indication of talent in these departments—there is a good chance that without realizing it you do want to succeed in terms of salary. If this is the case, the first job you pick is not as important from the viewpoint of interest as it is from the viewpoint of opportunity. The answer, in fact, may be very obvious. A rather rounded person (I can't believe you're completely spherical) with no dominant interest often makes an excellent salesman. I have frequently predicted that salesmen are going to be very important factors in American business in the decades to come.

I have a moderate inheritance—about $100,000. I have an opportunity to invest it in a small local business in which

171

I will also serve as a junior executive. Will being a stock-holder give me an advantage when competing for promotions?

None whatsoever. Unless you have experience that the company needs, investing your money in it will have nothing to do with advancing you. Profit margins are too narrow in business today to tolerate drones, and no one is going to give you a raise just to keep you and your investment around. If the company needs the money in order to stay solvent, that is an even better reason not to invest it. You would be far wiser to take the job, keep your money in the bank or in the market, and study the company closely for a year or so. Then, with mature judgment, if you think the company is worth the risk, put your money into it, without illusions about red-carpeting your way to the president's chair.

I have a chance to take a job with a government agency, at the same salary ($13,500) I am getting now. Will the experience be valuable to me in business?

It will probably hurt you more than help you. At the very top, government experience can help a man's business career. But the men who get these jobs have already succeeded fairly well in the business world. Your job is obviously in the middle range, and I can think of nothing that a government agency can give you at that level that a challenging job in industry would not give you, faster and more effectively. In fact you can learn some very bad budgetary habits and even worse personnel practices in government, habits that could ruin you forever in industry. If you feel motivated to go into government to serve your country, I applaud. We need talented, dedicated people in government. But if your goal in life is substantial success in the business world, avoid government work until they come looking for you.

I want to work overseas, not only because the life appeals to me, but because I understand the opportunities are better.

You are wrong about the opportunities. Like many people, you have been misled by reading reports of the billions American companies are investing overseas. The reports are true, but in most cases even the executives, right up to (and sometimes including) the president, are chosen from the foreign country. American industry has become very sensitive to propaganda attacks on it and is going out of the way to prove we are not economic imperialists. As a result, the opportunities overseas, far from expanding, are actually dwindling at present. At least for Americans they are. I get a fairly large number of requests for marketing executives for overseas jobs. But almost always the company specifies they want an Englishman. If that makes you mad, don't blame me. The trouble starts in Moscow.

What's the most interesting business idea you've come across recently?

In England, of all places, Thurrock Technical College has concocted a program which uses students as "sales cadets." The idea has given many small, somewhat moribund businesses a chance to make contact with bright, talented, aggressive young people, who are bubbling with the latest techniques and eager to try a few of their own. Thurrock has sent these kids to Copenhagen, Vienna, and Zurich to sell for these firms, and they have racked up astonishing records. They are now about to expand to West Germany and Italy. Maybe the moral is, when you've got your back to the wall, as the English jolly well have, you do your best thinking.

My husband sells life insurance. He makes about $20,000 a year and lives a happy-go-lucky, relaxed life, taking many days off to fish and hunt and hike in the woods and mountains near our home. Friends tell me that with his personality and intelligence he could make $40,000 to $50,000 working for a corporation. Should I push him to change jobs?

Probably not. I'm not against wives pushing husbands. It sometimes gives a good man the extra bit of fire he needs to go all the way to the top. But your husband sounds like he would be miserable in the structured world of the corporation. I'm sure that everybody who buys insurance from him considers him a friend. But in the corporation, friendship does not go very far, especially today. A man like your husband would almost certainly find the brutal competition a terrific strain, and he would probably miss the outdoor life he loves. You might find yourself married to an entirely different person—and not very happily married at that.

I'm a young executive. Will my liberal politics affect my chances for promotion?

There is a standard answer to this question. Of course not, our corporations believe in the American tradition of free political choice, etc., etc. Now I will give you *my* answer.

Yes, definitely, and more so in the years to come. Fewer and fewer executives are going to tolerate (much less promote) people around them who favor the company-destroying, profit-denying policies of the liberal left. There is a mounting sense of frustration among business leaders at the seemingly deliberate hostility so many politicians and government servants display toward business. In a war for survival, those who are not with the businessman are against him. This, regrettably, is what a lot of top executives are beginning to believe. So you can hardly expect them to promote you if you are loudly supporting political policies which they view as destructive to business and businessmen.

THE ESSENCE
OF SUCCESS

ONE question has recurred with almost dependable regularity both in my mail and at the many talks I give to business and college groups. "If you had to sum up the secret of success in a single sentence, what would you say?"

At first I floundered. I fell back on clichés such as drive and ambition. I even threw a fish to luck. I sought for the answer in Professor McClelland's researches. But a born maverick can't accept another man's answers, illuminating though they may be. So one day I sat down and studied my own career. All of the clichés were operative at first glance: hard work, the ambition that drives every man who has experienced poverty. Luck was involved, more than once. But gradually I saw in the pattern I had instinctively evolved another principle.

I do not consider myself one of the world's great geniuses. I have an average amount of energy and an average amount of brains. But I have parlayed them into a reasonable facsimile of success by using an old idea in a new way.

If you can't be first, be a little different.

Suddenly I realized how many successful men I knew had used the same approach. It is, I am now convinced, the heart and soul of the success stories you see in *Business Week* and *Forbes* and *Fortune*, and it also applies to the stories you don't read about, the man who makes a very comfortable living out of a retail store or a small chain of franchises, a local public relations agency, or a brokerage firm. In fact, we hear too much about the guys who are first, the front-runners who roll up the $500-million-conglomerates. We don't hear enough about why Joe Smith manages the most profitable supermarket in town, and why Joe Brown's store is going broke. I would be willing to bet the explanation is in that word "different."

It's equally true for the line or staff executive in a larger company. Too often he thinks, after plowing through dozens of how-to books, "I'd better just treadmill along. I don't have any original ideas." So at conferences he sits back and lets a maverick dominate the scene. Most of the time, the maverick's ideas are no more original than his own. But the maverick is different enough to push himself into the limelight, and often that's all it takes. Or he knows how to present commonplace thoughts with style and verve.

When the psychologists discuss this idea they call it creativity. I don't like the word myself, it smacks too much of the bizarre, the world of art. But the psychologists argue that the impulse to do something differently in business, or in anything else, including how to raise your children, is essentially the same thing that motivates a man to paint a picture or write a novel. Moreover, the psychologists say everybody has some of this creativity in them. No matter how long a man has been plodding along on the treadmill, he has a spark of it in him somewhere. And he can let it out, I think, if he stops swallowing other men's how-to's and starts regularly repeating that slogan.

Maybe I can't be first, but I can be a little different.